# Manifest with the Moon
# Astro-Moon Journal 2024

from the I Choose Love Series.
The Pathway of the Spiritual Warrior.

# Manifest with the Moon
# Astro-Moon Journal 2024

This Journal Belongs to

_______________________________________________

Manifest with the Moon Astro-Moon Journal 2024
From the I Choose Love Series
The Pathway of the Spiritual Warrior

Manifest with the Moon Astro-Moon Diary & Journal
The Art of Manifestation Astro-Moon Diary & Journal
First Published 2019 A-Z of Emotional Health Ltd.

Published by the A-Z of Emotional Health Ltd.


isbn - 978-1-8382863-9-2

## Contents

# Manifest with the Moon

# Astro-Moon Journal 2024

For extra Moon information & webinars follow Jenny on social media

- https://www.youtube.com/c/MoonMagicWeeklyTarot
- https://www.facebook.com/MoonMagicJennyFlorence
- https://www.instagram.com/moonmagicjennyflorence/

# The Wisdom and Teachings of the Moon

Science tells us that what you are thinking and feeling, right here and right now, is creating and influencing the shape of your world, both now and into the future. But life doesn't always run smoothly... and when the tough stuff lands it can be really hard to keep your cool and hold onto a positive outlook, let alone feel as though you have any influence or agency over the circumstances that are going on around you.

Having worked as an Accredited UK registered Counsellor for over 28 years, I know from real hands on experience that regardless of what has taken place and is taking place in our lives, we can navigate through and beyond difficulties and challenges, and come out thriving... but we need the tools to do so... and in my search to discover anything and everything that can help people to navigate life better, and with greater empowerment, I found myself learning about the influence of the Moon.

Now I am someone who likes to be very hands on... I don't just want to read about something, I want to actually do it and see how it works for myself, and I can genuinely tell you that learning about the influence of the Moon and then discovering how the Lunar energy was affecting me personally has been a life transforming experience. In fact, every aspect of my world has changed for the better!

Many studies have shown that having a connection with nature is profoundly valuable in maintaining your health, physically, mentally, emotionally, and spiritually. I have discovered that living in alignment with the Moon is a truly magical experience, it puts you in touch with the natural world and actually teaches you to listen to your own real experience, and to find your own rhythm... and when the big stuff happens, even if you have a wobble, the knowledge of what's happening with the Moon will throw you an anchor, get you regrounded, and put you back on track.

And this is what inspired me to create the Manifest with the Moon Astro-Moon Diary. The diary is a tool to give you all the information you need to navigate your world with awareness of the incoming influence of the Moon and to learn how this affects you personally.

But being me... I wanted to learn more... and so, as a part of my Lunar investigations, I started to read about the Celtic and Pagan Tree Lore traditions and the stories and teachings that are associated with the different Moon cycles of the year, and I was then introduced to the Thirteen Native American Tribal Clan Moon Mothers through the writings of Jamie Sams, taking my understanding of the teachings of the Moon to a whole new level.

When I started to explore and read the monthly teachings, ongoing, I was absolutely stunned to realize that during each Moon month, the kinds of circumstances that were consistently arriving in my life aligned perfectly with the life lessons and spiritual growth that were being presented in these ancient wisdom traditions... and that the teachings were bringing me exactly the perspectives that I needed to find the undercurrent of deeper learning, regardless of what was going on.

And curiously... I realized that I was not alone in this... even within the uniqueness of different people's individual situations, I was seeing exactly the same kinds of life lessons mirrored in the life circumstances of my friends, my family, and my counselling clients alike!

And so, I began to see the Moon as a great teacher, whose monthly 'tutorial' could help me to view the challenges and the ups and downs of my world through a more grounded and objective lens. It was as though the Moon had become the mentor of my Soul supporting my human evolution and the highest growth possible from within any situation. And that is what led me to create this journal.

The Manifest with the Moon Astro-Moon Diary will teach you how to listen to the influence of the Moon on a day-to-day basis, with guided astrological information for all the Moon phases during every calendar month, whereas in this this journal, I share a deeper layer of learning that draws from tribal and wisdom traditions that honor living with respect and in relationship with nature and the Earth.

I am deeply indebted to the extraordinary work of Jamie Sams, whose gifted storytelling and profound wisdom opened up a whole new layer of growth and learning that for me has been lifechanging. I also wish to honor the work of Jan Spiller whose insightful work enabled me to really connect with the empowerment of the heightened energy at the New and Full Moons.

At the end of this journal I have compiled a reading list of the books that have informed my learning and united my spiritual beliefs with my therapeutic experience, and compounded my belief that every life experience, the good, the bad and everything in between, is actually an entry point into newer and higher levels of consciousness.

## How to Use this Journal

This journal will teach you about the life lessons and deeper growth and learning associated with the thirteen Moons of the year, enhancing your ability to become a conscious and active participant in manifesting the world that you wish to create, not only for yourself, but for future generations yet to come.

A Moon Month begins at each New Moon marking the beginning of a new Lunar phase of guidance, and so this journal is divided into thirteen sections with key Moon dates listed for the Moon month ahead, and I have found that there is a natural flow between the teachings, rather like a handover from one tutor to another with the influence of each Moon tutorial building upon the last.

And as the Lunar influence tends to be more concentrated at the time of the New and Full Moons, with the Quarter Moons bringing a natural point of evaluation and reflection, the journal is laid out around these Lunar focal points, with dedicated space to write your New Moon Wishes and Intentions, your Full Moon revelations and insights, and your Quarter Moon reflections and reviews, and right at the beginning of the journal I've given detailed information about these influences, including the impact of Solar and Lunar Eclipses, and also information about the eight Earth festivals.

Each Moon month I've also drawn on the natural properties of a particular stone or crystal that aligns with the Lunar energy each month, with information about how these natural healers of the Earth can aid and support you.

# The New, Full, and Quarter Moons

## The New Moon

Each New Moon marks the beginning of a new Lunar phase of teachings and a new chapter of evolution and manifestation. The natural world does not operate with abrupt divisions between days weeks months and years, the universe dances in beautiful mathematical patterns that beautifully integrate and are all consistent with a natural flow and momentum. In just the same way each set of teachings will flow from one into another, with each set of learnings building on the layer before.

New Moons are traditionally associated with the setting of wishes and intentions and so the energy at this time naturally invites us to meditate into a space of possibility. If you are a daily meditator, or a natural daydreamer, you may already find that for a couple of days before and sometimes a few days after the New Moon, your mind will tend to wander. You may also find that your sleeping dreams are more prolific and more detailed. I find it really helpful to keep a pen and paper with me at this time, or a recording device, so I can make a note of any visions, thoughts, and ideas, as they arrive.

Whilst frequently spoken of together, New Moon wishes, and New Moon intentions are actually different. A wish is embodied by the energy of the feminine and calls from the heart, inviting us to enter an internal creative space, and from within this dreamtime, formulate a clarity of desire. Whereas an intention is embodied by the masculine and asks us to formulate clear decisions that create pathways of action in the external world to move our dreams and desires into form.

Whatever your preferred way of finding stillness, calm your mind, and enter your own dreamtime. Let your mind wander into the depths of the New Moon energy... this is like a period of spiritual brainstorming... then take time to meditate further on your wishes before formulating your intended courses of action.

The timing for the setting of your wishes and intentions is actually very precise as the energy is strongest from the exact point of connection between the Moon and the Sun, gradually diminishing in the following eight hours, and this is the energy we want to tap into when we make our New Moon wishes and intentions.

For the few days before the New Moon, use the slowing down of the Lunar influence to lean into the dreamtime energy with plenty of time allocated for journaling and the preparation of your wishes and intentions, then with the New Moon energy at its most powerful, set your wishes and intentions during the eight hours following the exact time of the New Moon in your location. Exact timings across the globe are listed for each New Moon.

## The First Quarter Moon

Every quarter Moon is a point of balance between the magnetic pull of both the Sun and the Moon and although this connection is not entirely without tension, the Lunar influence at this time creates a space of natural review, so take time to press the pause button and become an observer of your circumstances.

The energy of the Moon is now building and gathering momentum... we see her getting bigger and bigger by the day, so this is a great time to consider how and where you intend to channel and invest this growing expanding energy.

Look at where you are in your manifestations and your personal learning. What is showing up in your world right now? What is calling for your attention, and what do you need to prioritize? Where should you apply your greatest focus? And depending on the Lunar lessons of the month, what are you being shown that will support your greatest and highest path of expanding awareness? This is a magnificent time to journal with focus!

What kind of work will need to be done to nurture your dreams into real form? Whether you are contemplating inner or outer areas of your world... whether you are building something new or investing in an ongoing project/venture/relationship... get focused and consider in real terms what you need to do to prioritize and to formulate your actions and move ahead.

Onwards and upwards!

## The Full Moon

When the Moon is Full the Sun, and the Moon are sitting directly opposite each other with the Earth... and therefore us too... bang in the middle!

This is a time of highly charged Lunar energy when we often experience heightened and intense emotions... but there is purpose to this and with the right knowledge and awareness you can align with this energy to enhance your growth, your learning, and your progression.

For several days before reaching her fullest, the Lunar energy will build, and with a noticeable intensity, so make a conscious choice to be kind to yourself and others. The brightness of this powerful Moon phase brings a space of authenticity where all is revealed and illuminated... so notice and listen! It is also highly likely that circumstances that are pushed to the fore of your world at this time will be offering life lessons that align with the Moon tutorial of the month.

The Full Moon illuminates exactly what is working... as well as anything that is not... and for most of us it is often a mixture of both! Stuff in your life that is on track will get a turbo charged boost of clarity with renewed energy to persevere and stay the course, but anything that is out of balance and not okay, especially the stuff that you might have been trying to ignore or sweep under the carpet, will surface, and request your attention. So, if you find yourself experiencing any challenging emotions please take them seriously.

At the highest peak of intensity when the Full Moon is exact, immediately afterwards there is a release point, a breathing out and a letting go, and you can actively use this release point to enhance ceremonies of cleansing and releasing, so you can then move forwards with clarity... in mind, emotion, body, and Soul!

So... in the build up to this peak of energy, consciously create pockets of time to get still... notice and listen... and use your journaling time to reflect and ask for clarity. Then at the point of shift, release and let go, and with cleanness of energy and clarity of mind, continue on your way with steady momentum.

If at this point you are in any way uncertain as to the next steps ahead, continue to journal with an emphasis on seeking answers from within. If you're stuck or struggling to move forwards, it is often an aspect of the past that is still lingering, creating limiting beliefs and automatic responses that are getting in the way. When the Moon reaches her last quarter position the Lunar influence naturally creates an inward space of review and much inward clarity can be gained through ongoing internal enquiry at this time.

If you work with healing stones and crystals, the Full Moon is like a crystal battery charger, so be sure to place your crystals outside overnight to revitalize and recharge their energy for the coming month. You may also want to place some rainwater or spring water in a bowl and leave it out overnight to absorb the energy of the Full Moon. Do NOT use a plastic bowl! Use glass or earthenware or any container whose fundamental ingredients come from a natural source.

Your Moon water will carry the qualities of the Zodiac sign that the Full Moon is in, as well as the healing energy of that month's Lunar lessons, so store it in a labelled jar and use it for healing and in your ceremonies throughout the year.

## The Last Quarter Moon

The magnetic pull of the Sun and the Moon is again at an equal point creating a balance of energy between the outgoing creativity and thrust of the masculine and the internal reflective evaluation and nurture of the feminine. As the Moon is now becoming smaller the energy asks you pause and do a check in to see if your external circumstances are in alignment with your internal values.

The Full Moon energy gave you an opportunity to see what you needed to move ahead, including the things you needed to let go of. The energy of the Last Quarter Moon is now inviting you to consolidate your progress and evaluate.

Are any unwanted patterns still repeating? Are your plans, actions, and decisions congruent with all that you wish to be and all that you wish to see in the world? Are you really honoring your truest values and deepest desires? What do you need to nurture for it to move along? Do you need to stand firm, or do you need to course correct?

The last quarter Moon marks a turning point and a shift in momentum. Between now and the New Moon the energy is slowing down, and consistency with slow and steady will win the race... plus ample opportunity to make adjustments along the way... and most importantly, to remember to stop and smell the roses!

What we actually have is NOW and when we get to tomorrow it will be NOW!

So integrate your learning and follow it through, cross any T's or dot any I's and get present enough to notice, are you 'being' everything that you wish to attract for yourself... for example, how positive are your thoughts? Does your inner critic offer constructive feedback or harsh criticism? Are you kinder to others than to yourself? ... or is it the other way around?

This is a magnificent time to journal in anticipation of setting clear and deeply personal New Moon wishes and intentions.

Inwards and upwards!

## Solar and Lunar Eclipses

During eclipse season, the already intense energy of both the New and Full Moons are intensified. An eclipse in your sign, will often be a significant trigger point or turning point in your own personal process of evolution and can often herald random events that create sudden and unexpected changes.

On your personal journey of manifestation, understanding this heightened and intensified energy is incredibly helpful in knowing when to reflect and set your intentions, and when to take action to move something forwards, particularly if you intend to make or initiate significant changes in any aspect of your life.

Eclipses are also associated with our Karmic journey, creating an energetic rift that overrides our usual perception of and connection to time. The energy of the eclipses is said to open an energetic portal that connects past, present, and future, highlighting your purpose and calling in this present lifetime.

Symbolized in the tarot pack by the cards of Death and the Tower, the energy of both the solar and lunar eclipses are associated with transformation, either internally or in the circumstances of our external lives, and often involves both endings and new beginnings.

I think the best way to work with the influence of the eclipses, is rather than trying to control events, consciously make time to slow down, get still, and practice the art of allowing... let the Universe show you the way, whilst being responsive and taking action as needed.

### Solar Eclipse

A solar eclipse is when the Moon sits in between the Sun and the Earth, with the Moon covering the Sun. This will always occur at a New Moon. The energy associated with this time is the same as a New Moon, but intensified, like a New Moon on steroids!

This is the perfect time to get still and to meditate into a space of personal dreamtime and allow your ideas to flow.

The energy of the solar eclipse can bring an extraordinary surge of creative possibilities, although these may not always arrive in the shape or form that you expect, so if you're already involved in setting wishes and intentions, but then find that something happens to suddenly create a shift in your direction, trust that this unexpected change is important to your personal growth and evolution and connected to the calling of your soul. In matters of manifestation, the universe will always have the upper hand and tends to bring us what we need... although not always what we want!

When you can trust that even in moments of upheaval and disruption you are being gifted with an opportunity, you open yourself to receive the fullest potential and the greatest learning to be found in every situation.

### Lunar Eclipse

A lunar eclipse is when the earth sits between the Moon and the Sun, and this will always occur at a Full Moon. Full Moons are associated with heightened emotions and during a lunar eclipse, emotions can run high, like a Full Moon on steroids!

If we think of the Moon as our Feminine Guardian who circles our planet, gathering the energy of the Sun and redistributing it to the Earth in various measures, at the time of a Lunar Eclipse, the energy of the Moon is like a fully charged battery, highly charged and ready to ignite change.

In the illumination of the Full Moon at her most powerful, all is revealed.

Anything and everything that is running smoothly and working in service of a balanced and authentic life will be apparent to you, confirming that you are walking the right path. Likewise, anything and everything that is not working for you or no longer serving you, both internally and externally, will also be brought into the light, calling to be addressed, changed, and if necessary, released.

As long as something remains hidden or unconscious, you are helpless to address the issue and to take actions of resolution, but when you identify a problem, the very fact that you can see the issue clearly creates an opportunity to seek solutions and find ways forward.

On your personal journey of manifestation, the energy of a lunar eclipse increases your connections with any emotional residue from the past that may be clinging and coloring your perspectives inappropriately, creating an amazing opportunity for cleansing and release, clearing the way for resolution and healing. This is a powerful time to embrace forgiveness, of both yourself and others.

If you are struggling with any difficult emotions this book will help you to understand your Emotions as a source of empowerment... yes... even the tough ones!

- Mindfulness meets Emotional Awareness - 7 Steps to Learn the Language of your Emotions - https://www.amazon.com/author/jennyflorence

Lunar eclipses are also often associated with external changes that are a mirror or a reflection of our internal growth and learning, so whatever is taking place around you, if something in your life appears to be needing to change or to leave, let go gracefully and know that it is timely to the evolution of your soul.

If you are naturally a highly empathic person and particularly sensitive to the feelings of others, at the time of a lunar eclipse you may find yourself highly absorbent of the emotional states of the people around you. Be sure to cleanse and do a daily release ceremony to let go of anything that doesn't belong to you before meditating into your own space of illumination.

- **25th March – Full Moon Lunar Eclipse - 05°07' Libra**
- **8th April –- New Moon Solar Eclipse - 19°23' Aries**
- **18th September – Full Moon Lunar Eclipse - 25°40' Pisces**
- **2nd October – New Moon Solar Eclipse - 10°03' Libra**

# The Earth Festivals

## The Natural Turning of the Seasons Celebrations and Ceremony

All of the Earth festivals are in essence a turning point and a natural marker in time, it is as though the Earth herself pauses for breath and the space between heaven and earth becomes fluid, translucent, and free of clutter.

These shifts in time and space open up access to higher levels of consciousness and awareness and I have found that if you slow down enough during the four-day window that surrounds these pivotal shifts in energy,
you can literally 'feel' the point of turn and the space of new emergence. It is a truly magical experience, and the perfect time to create ceremonies of intent for the coming season.

Over a four-day period, with two days either side of these powerful shifts, you may well experience much higher levels of intuition with a heightened ability to channel and connect with source energy, divine inspiration, and the greater collective consciousness.

In manifestation this is an incredible time to bring about shifts that free you from limiting beliefs, giving you a jump-start and a revitalization of energy and momentum.

No wonder our ancestors celebrated these markers in time in ceremony at sacred sites offering appreciation and gratitude to the Earth. This planet is our home, and this beautiful Earth gives to us unconditionally, ultimately providing us with everything that we need to physically live. Without her we cannot exist. The Earth festivals are an amazing opportunity to celebrate and honor your connection with the earth and all that she gives you right down to those core basic, simple, and yet essential things that sustain your very existence.

The Earth that you walk upon, the air you breath, the fire in your hearts and the water that not only sustains all of life but is so intimately connected with the energy and influence of our beautiful Moon. And providing your intent is genuine and your appreciation comes from the heart this actually creates a win/win situation!

Energetically, gratitude and appreciation are key tools in the law of attraction, holding a very high vibrational energy. When you offer genuine thanks to the Earth, you not only feed and fuel the energy and resonance of the Earth, but you also align yourself with the magnetic force of gratitude which will actually turbo charge your own wishes, desires, and manifestations.

## Earth Festival Dates 2024

- **Imbolc Northern Hemisphere – Lammas Southern Hemisphere. $1^{st}$ February.**
- **Spring Equinox Northern Hemisphere – Autumn Equinox Southern Hemisphere. $20^{th}$ March.**
- **Beltane Northern Hemisphere – Samhain Southern Hemisphere. $1^{st}$ May.**
- **Summer Solstice Northern Hemisphere – Winter Solstice Southern Hemisphere. $20^{th}$ June.**
- **Lammas Northern Hemisphere – Imbolc Southern Hemisphere. $1^{st}$ August.**
- **Autumn Equinox Northern Hemisphere – Spring Equinox Southern Hemisphere. $22^{nd}$ September.**
- **Samhain Northern Hemisphere – Beltane Southern Hemisphere. $31^{st}$ October.**
- **Winter Solstice Northern Hemisphere – Summer Solstice Southern Hemisphere. $21^{st}$ December.**

## Desires, Goals, and Intentions, for 2024

*Every life experience, the good, the bad and everything in between, is actually an entry point into newer and higher levels of consciousness.*

## Desires, Goals, and Intentions, for the Coming Month

## Moon Dates January into February

- New Moon in Capricorn - January 11/22
- First Quarter Moon in Taurus - January 18
- Full Moon in Leo - January 25/26
- Imbolc Northern Hemisphere – Lammas Southern Hemisphere – February 1
- Last Quarter Moon in Scorpio - February 2/3
- New Moon in Aquarius - February 9/10

## The First Moon Phase of 2024

### January 2024 / February 2024

### The Tree Lore of Birch and the First Moon Talks with Relations

***You are energy... I am energy... everything in this magnificent Universe is made of the same stuff... all interconnected... all one and the same!***

In January we move into the Moon time of Birch who in Tree Lore is the keeper of new beginnings and Talks with Relations. Following a forest fire the Birch is the first tree to seed itself, investing and committing fully to establish the beginnings of a whole new community. This is a tree whose teachings recognize that we each have a unique part to play and that every contribution brings value to the whole.

The wisdom of Talks with Relations taught me that everything is alive and that we are an integral part of the web of life. Her story explains how to live without judgement or competitive comparison and urges us to value difference as a source of profound learning. She teaches us that when we honor and respect all of life, we are also honoring ourselves.

During this Moon I found that many situations in my personal world were focused on family, community, and my closest relationships, and whilst some of the connections were amazing and wonderful, others were not so easy! The influence of Talks with Relations inspires a change of perspective, particularly within relationships recognizing that we all have a unique part to play.

So during this Moon time, to take time to consciously appreciate the unique pathways and contributions that everyone is making... even people who are difficult and challenging! Ironically these are the people who often teach us the most, contributing massively to our Soul growth and personal evolution... and appreciation holds a very high vibration! Now let's extend your relationships beyond your fellow human beings... connecting through love and respect with all your relations, not just your fellow human beings, but every living thing, opens up a depth of spiritual communication that is truly life changing. When you become still enough to truly listen, you open yourself to an incredible source of guidance and support and this level of connectedness will help you to maintain perspective and inspire you to act with the wellbeing of the whole, in mind.

During this Moon time invest in periods of stillness... especially at the turning point of Imbolc and Lammas, both festivals of fertility that call for investment and commitment, and if you need support reach out to all your relations and ask for it.

**Amazonite.**
**Aligning with the First Moon Phase Talks with Relations.**
**Inviting respect, equality, and truth.**

For me, Amazonite feels akin to the Tarot Card of Justice. It has a sense of gravity about it, calling us to stand in truth and walk a pathway of justice, equality, and fairness. And yet despite its powerful presence it radiates calm, coupled with an inner peace and an inner sense of deep wellbeing, fostering genuine self-esteem built on a foundation of honor and integrity.

It is said that the energy of Amazonite enables us to stand back and view our situation from all angles, supporting us in becoming an objective observer of life. Associated with the Heart Chakra it is said to enhance our ability to manifest through a deep interconnectedness with the universal love that flows through all of life.

***You are energy... I am energy... everything in this magnificent Universe is made of the same stuff... all interconnected... all one and the same!***

## The New Moon - January 11th / 12th - 20° 44' Capricorn

A Capricorn New Moon always falls in the period of the end of December through into the beginning of January and so this is perfect Moon for making wishes that focus on your New Year resolutions and intentions. Capricorn energy naturally focuses on ambitions, goals, and personal desires for success and recognition and so in your preparations for this Moon time you may want to ask yourself what really matters to you, and what have you learned from the previous year, and what do you wish to focus on and manifest in the year ahead?

The earthy pragmatic energy of Capricorn invites you to think about your long-term goals, and to take a structured approach to the potential that you wish to step into. So to use the energy at its absolute best take some time to review the past year, contemplate your future, then make a constructive pragmatic list of intentions that support your New Moon wishes and desires. You may also want to create a vision board with a clear focus on your ultimate goals for the coming year.

If you are aware of any inner blocks to your success, such as self-doubt or a lack of confidence, this is the perfect time to make wishes that support the release of any form of self-sabotaging thinking patterns or behaviors. This is also the perfect Moon to request guidance and information to align your ambitions with your true purpose and calling and to ask to be shown the next pragmatic and practical steps to manifest this into being.

In your New Moon ceremonies write down your 10 wishes and open yourself to receive the guidance that you need to highlight the next steps on your pathway of manifestation. To engage with the New Moon energy at its most powerful, be sure to write your wishes down during the 8 hours following the exact time of the New Moon in your location.

**New Moon Global Timings:**

- Los Angeles, USA — Thu, 11 Jan 2024 at 03:57 PST
- New York, USA — Thu, 11 Jan 2024 at 06:57 EST
- Reykjavik, Iceland — Thu, 11 Jan 2024 at 11:57 GMT
- London, UK — Thu, 11 Jan 2024 at 11:57 GMT
- Paris, France — Thu, 11 Jan 2024 at 12:57 CET
- Cape Town, South Africa — Thu, 11 Jan 2024 at 13:57 SAST
- Delhi, India — Thu, 11 Jan 2024 at 17:27 IST
- Perth, Australia — Thu, 11 Jan 2024 at 19:57 AWST
- Tokyo, Japan — Thu, 11 Jan 2024 at 20:57 JST
- Sydney, Australia — Thu, 11 Jan 2024 at 22:57 AEDT
- Auckland, New Zealand — Fri, 12 Jan 2024 at 00:57 NZDT
- Greenwich Mean Time — Thu, 11 Jan 2024 at 11:57 GMT

## My Ten New Moon Wishes

*The First Moon Phase - Birch Moon – Talks with Relations*
*My Wishes and Dreams*

1

2

3

4

5

6

7

8

9

10

## My Ten New Moon Intentions

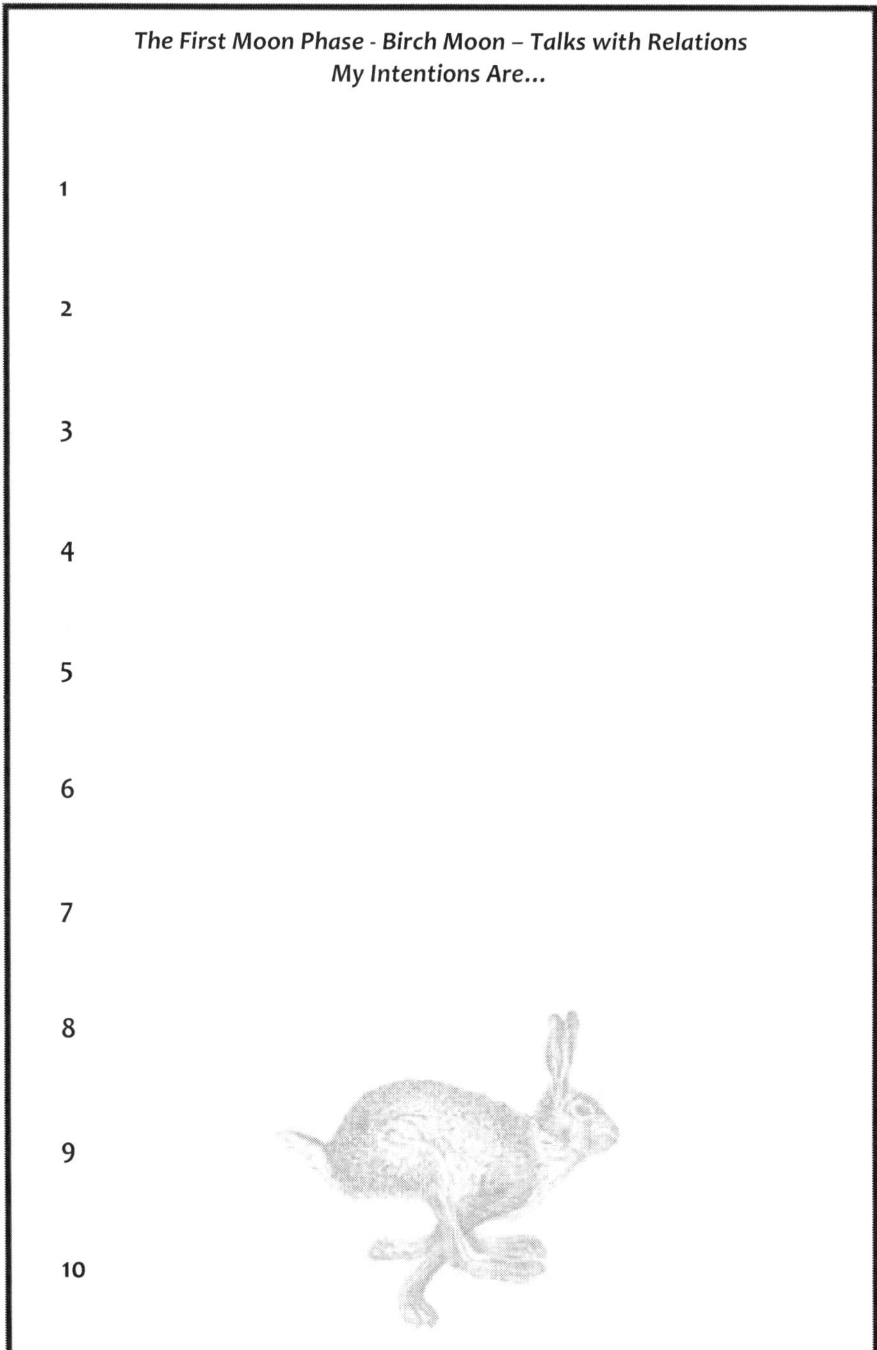

*The First Moon Phase - Birch Moon – Talks with Relations*
*My Intentions Are...*

1

2

3

4

5

6

7

8

9

10

## Journaling and Notes

***Learning to love and respect all your relations, not just your fellow human beings, but every living thing, opens up a depth of spiritual communication that is truly life changing.***

## My First Quarter Moon Thoughts and Reviews

### The First Quarter Moon – January 18th – Taurus

*The energy of the Moon is now building and gathering momentum… we see her getting bigger and bigger by the day, so this is a great time to consider how and where you intend to channel and invest this growing expanding energy.*

*Look at where you are in your manifestations and your personal learning. What is showing up in your world right now? What is calling for your attention, and what do you need to prioritize? Where should you apply your greatest focus?*

## The Full Moon - January 25th / 26th - 5° 14' Leo

A Full Moon in Leo naturally invites you to embrace exactly where you are, right here and right now, and to get present. I think that one of the best ways to use this energy is to lean into a space of celebration, take time out to play and to recharge your batteries, whilst also making a note of all that is shown to you at this time.

So if your world is feeling on track then celebrate, shout it to the world... or at very least to yourself... surf the waves or lie on the beach and take in the rays... whatever chills you out and works for you. But if any aspect of your life feels unsatisfactory then listen up and take your passions seriously! The Leo energy is here to help you to identify whatever is holding you back, whether this is internal stuff or situations that are taking place around you.

If you are experiencing any kind of conflict between your ego mind and the desires of your heart, the influence of Leo will support you in finding the courage to connect with your inner voice and to break free from any inappropriate restrictions and limitations that are getting in the way, both inner and outer.

Each month place some rainwater or spring water in a bowl and leave it out overnight to absorb the energy of the Full Moon. Do NOT use a plastic bowl! Use glass or earthenware or any container whose fundamental ingredients come from a natural source. Collect the water afterwards and store it in a jar. Use this Moon Water in ceremonies of celebration, commitment, and joy and also in situations where you are overcoming restrictions, being bold, seeking courage or needing to find your voice.

**Full Moon Global Timings:**

- Los Angeles, USA — Thu, 25 Jan 2024 at 09:53 PST
- New York, USA — Thu, 25 Jan 2024 at 12:53 EST
- Reykjavik, Iceland — Thu, 25 Jan 2024 at 17:53 GMT
- London, UK — Thu, 25 Jan 2024 at 17:53 GMT
- Paris, France — Thu, 25 Jan 2024 at 18:53 CET
- Cape Town, South Africa — Thu, 25 Jan 2024 at 19:53 SAST
- Delhi, India — Thu, 25 Jan 2024 at 23:23 IST
- Perth, Australia — Fri, 26 Jan 2024 at 01:53 AWST
- Tokyo, Japan — Fri, 26 Jan 2024 at 02:53 JST
- Sydney, Australia — Fri, 26 Jan 2024 at 04:53 AEDT
- Auckland, New Zealand — Fri, 26 Jan 2024 at 06:53 NZDT
- Greenwich Mean Time — Thu, 25 Jan 2024 at 17:53 GMT

## My Full Moon Insights and Illuminations

*The First Moon Phase - Birch Moon – Talks with Relations*

## Journaling and Notes

***Living with love and respect for all of life will bring an abundance of love and respect straight back to you.***

## My Last Quarter Moon Thoughts and Evaluations

### The Last Quarter Moon – February 2nd / 3rd – Scorpio

*The Last Quarter Moon invites you to consolidate your progress and evaluate. Are any unwanted patterns still repeating? Are your plans, actions, and decisions congruent with all that you wish to be and all that you wish to see in the world?*

*The last quarter Moon marks a turning point and a shift in momentum. This is a magnificent time to journal in anticipation of setting clear and deeply personal New Moon wishes and intentions.*

## Journaling and Notes

*If you can quiet your mind enough to notice, listen, and hear, you will discover there is an infinite source of guidance all around you.*

## Journaling and Notes

*The First Moon Phase - Birch Moon – Talks with Relations*

## Desires, Goals, and Intentions, for the Coming Month

## Moon Dates February into March

- New Moon in Aquarius - February 9/10
- First Quarter Moon in Taurus – February 16
- Full Moon in Virgo - February 24/25
- Last Quarter Moon in Sagittarius - March 3
- New Moon in Pisces – March 10

# The Second Moon Phase of 2024

## February 2024 / March 2024

## The Tree Lore of Rowan and the Second Moon Wisdom Keeper

***Find Liberation through Learning... Transform your Past Experiences into Wisdom... and Become Fully Present to both Give and Receive.***

In this month of learning we move to the influence of Rowan, the Tree of Life, whose qualities are associated with courage, wisdom, and protection, and the Moon of Wisdom Keeper. In the last Moon month, with respect and appreciation, you affirmed your relationship with all your relations and all of life. In this Moon time you get to look at the stuff that could be getting in the way of you staying on track. It's time to process your past experiences and transform them into wisdom and awareness, and the energy of Rowan bring the courage and safety to do this. If you find yourself having a wobble, try carrying a Rowan leaf with you. (Although please ask the tree first!)

You cannot change the past, but you can learn from it. Pretty much everyone I have ever met has some sort of internal belief or block within them that springs from the past, coloring their perceptions and attitudes. This is the stuff of humanness. The Moon of Wisdom Keeper invites you to honor the past without being bound by it. This Moon time brought me experiences that reminded me of the importance of keeping history alive, not in ways that caused me to remain entrenched or stuck in the past, but in ways that helped me to grow from past experiences. I also deepened my acceptance of the pathways of others, with an understanding of how much I could learn from the point of views of others.

When we can learn from every experience, even the most challenging ones, we become liberated from past perceptions and limitations, and can embrace the future with greater vision. I don't know about you, but the people I admire and respect the most are people who genuinely live with honor and integrity. They never use fear or manipulation as tools to wield power but lead through example... and often very quietly! Interestingly, all of these people have had to deal to deal with some pretty big stuff in their lives, and yet despite these experiences, they are better, stronger, and wiser. They are an inspiration and show that we all have this potential within us.

So, make a personal choice to become your own hero or heroine... slow down, learn to listen, and become an observer, particularly of your internal world and your own responses. See yourself as the source of change within your own world and as you release inner blocks and become stronger and wiser you will be a role model to others who struggle with similar issues.

## Green Calcite.
## Aligning with the Second Moon Phase Wisdom Keeper.
## Remembering brings healing and resolution.

Green Calcite is sometimes known as a memory stone. Aligning with the Heart Chakra and the Higher Heart Chakra, its energy supports healing within the emotional, spiritual, physical, and mental realms, thus offering opportunity to assist in the resolution of any historic or challenging memories, freeing us from the past through awareness and understanding.

I find that when I sit with this gorgeous crystal, I automatically begin to view my situation differently, and in overriding past perspectives, I can hold past memories in a far more objective and forgiving light. In meditation this crystal is said to open channels of communication with our ancestors, bringing guidance, healing, and wisdom.

***Find Liberation through Learning... Transform your Past Experiences into Wisdom... and Become Fully Present to both Give and Receive.***

## The New Moon – February 9th / 10th - 20° 40' Aquarius

The energy of an Aquarius New Moon is the perfect time to make wishes and intentions that hold a higher vision for humanity, and the timing of this Moon lends itself perfectly to focus on bringing higher love, and greater purpose to all areas of your personal life as well as a vision of peace for the greater collective. Because this is the Moon of Lunar Imbolc in the Northern Hemisphere, marking a pivotal turn of Earth magic, this is a time when the overall energy flow is absolutely loaded with fertility.

So use this New Moon to make wishes that support and enhance your vision for the coming year and start to get really specific about the details!

If your life is already feeling on track then lean into a space of excited anticipation… align your desires with a purpose that stretches beyond your own immediate needs… dare to dream big… and then set your wishes accordingly! If however, there is any form of uncertainty or apprehension about your pathway, or events and circumstances seem to be pushing you to evaluate and restructure some aspect of your life, then empty your mind of pre-conceptions… lean into the higher energy of potential contribution and service… and set wishes that ask for illumination and guidance.

In your New Moon ceremonies write down your 10 wishes and open yourself to receive the guidance that you need to highlight the next steps on your pathway of manifestation.

To engage with the New Moon energy at its most powerful, be sure to write your wishes down during the 8 hours following the exact time of the New Moon in your location.

**New Moon Global Timings:**

- Los Angeles, USA — Fri, 9 Feb 2024 at 14:58 PST
- New York, USA — Fri, 9 Feb 2024 at 17:58 EST
- Reykjavik, Iceland — Fri, 9 Feb 2024 at 22:58 GMT
- London, UK — Fri, 9 Feb 2024 at 22:58 GMT
- Paris, France — Fri, 9 Feb 2024 at 23:58 CET
- Cape Town, South Africa — Sat, 10 Feb 2024 at 00:58 SAST
- Delhi, India — Sat, 10 Feb 2024 at 04:28 IST
- Perth, Australia — Sat, 10 Feb 2024 at 06:58 AWST
- Tokyo, Japan — Sat, 10 Feb 2024 at 07:58 JST
- Sydney, Australia — Sat, 10 Feb 2024 at 09:58 AEDT
- Auckland, New Zealand — Sat, 10 Feb 2024 at 11:58 NZDT
- Greenwich Mean Time — Fri, 9 Feb 2024 at 22:58 GMT

## My Ten New Moon Wishes

*The Second Moon Phase - Rowan Moon - Wisdom Keeper*
*My Wishes and Dreams*

1

2

3

4

5

6

7

8

9

10

## My Ten New Moon Intentions

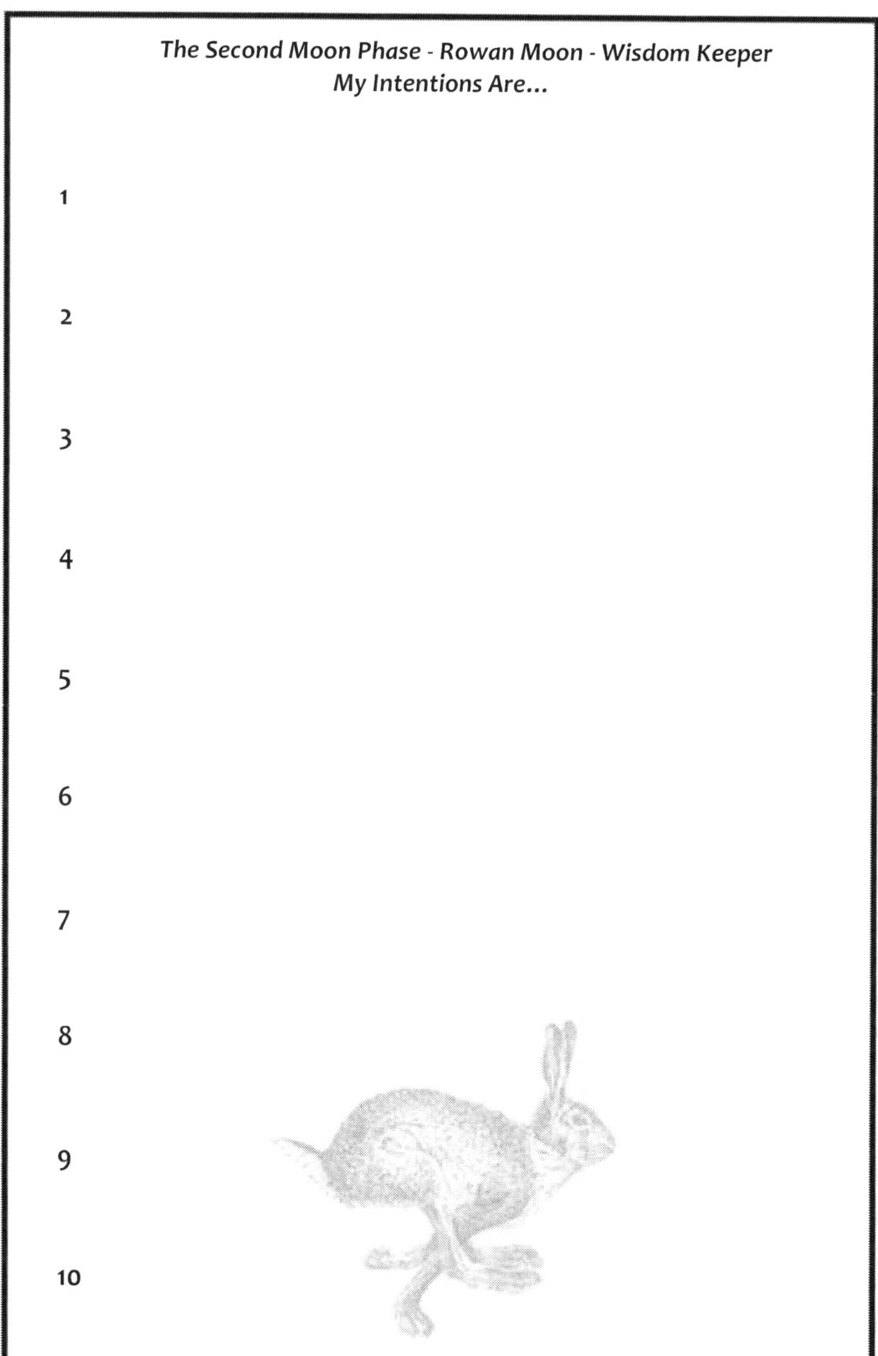

*The Second Moon Phase - Rowan Moon - Wisdom Keeper*
*My Intentions Are...*

1

2

3

4

5

6

7

8

9

10

## Journaling and Notes

*In this Moon time you get to look at the stuff that could be getting in the way of you staying on track, whilst also learning to maintain your vision.*

## My First Quarter Moon Thoughts and Reviews

### The First Quarter Moon – February 16th – Taurus

*The energy of the Moon is now building and gathering momentum… we see her getting bigger and bigger by the day, so this is a great time to consider how and where you intend to channel and invest this growing expanding energy.*

*Look at where you are in your manifestations and your personal learning. What is showing up in your world right now? What is calling for your attention, and what do you need to prioritize? Where should you apply your greatest focus?*

## The Full Moon - February 24th / 25th - 5° 22' Virgo

A Full Moon in Virgo, brings the prefect energetic to review and attend to the details, seeing every aspect of a situation before diligently following through with actions that support powerful transformation for the benefit of all. Wherever you are on your personal journey of manifestation, there is a wonderful flow of energy available today bringing opportunity for healing through practical action. Whether you are reaching some form of completion, birthing something new into the world, or moving into the next phase of an ongoing project/ situation/ relationship, the energy of this powerful Full Moon in Virgo is an invitation to scrutinize, evaluate, get clear, and move forwards from a position of renewed clarity. Now... if anything emerges at this time that requires change, and you happen to have a raging inner critic, then please do not pick yourself (or indeed anyone else) to pieces. This is a Moon that invites change through awareness, so whatever is uppermost in your world invest with integrity, pay attention to the details, do the work, and trust that the right doorways are going to open! Areas of personal conflict, with a particular focus around themes of; the needs of others versus the needs of ourselves; self-care or care of others; inappropriate levels of obligation versus realistic support of others; etc.. could well surface at this time with a call to address any imbalances both internally and externally, moving circumstances and situations into a space of transformation, completion, and re-birth.
Each month place some rainwater or spring water in a bowl and leave it out overnight to absorb the energy of the Full Moon. Do NOT use a plastic bowl! Use glass or earthenware or any container whose fundamental ingredients come from a natural source. Collect the water afterwards and store it in a jar.
Use this Moon Water in any of your ceremonies that help to heal and rebalance any aspect of inner criticism and promote actions that require diligence and consistency with attention to detail.

**Full Moon Global Timings:**

- Los Angeles, USA — Sat, 24 Feb 2024 at 04:30 PST
- New York, USA — Sat, 24 Feb 2024 at 07:30 EST
- Reykjavik, Iceland — Sat, 24 Feb 2024 at 12:30 GMT
- London, UK — Sat, 24 Feb 2024 at 12:30 GMT
- Paris, France — Sat, 24 Feb 2024 at 13:30 CET
- Cape Town, South Africa — Sat, 24 Feb 2024 at 14:30 SAST
- Delhi, India — Sat, 24 Feb 2024 at 18:00 IST
- Perth, Australia — Sat, 24 Feb 2024 at 20:30 AWST
- Tokyo, Japan — Sat, 24 Feb 2024 at 21:30 JST
- Sydney, Australia — Sat, 24 Feb 2024 at 23:30 AEDT
- Auckland, New Zealand — Sun, 25 Feb 2024 at 01:30 NZDT
- Greenwich Mean Time — Sat, 24 Feb 2024 at 12:30 GMT

## My Full Moon Insights and Illuminations

## Journaling and Notes

*The people I admire and respect the most are people who genuinely live with honor and integrity. They never use fear or manipulation as tools to wield power but lead through example... and often very quietly!*

## My Last Quarter Moon Thoughts and Evaluations

### The Last Quarter Moon – March 3rd – Sagittarius

*The Last Quarter Moon invites you to consolidate your progress and evaluate. Are any unwanted patterns still repeating? Are your plans, actions, and decisions congruent with all that you wish to be and all that you wish to see in the world?*

*The last quarter Moon marks a turning point and a shift in momentum. This is a magnificent time to journal in anticipation of setting clear and deeply personal New Moon wishes and intentions.*

## Journaling and Notes

***Make a personal choice to become your own hero or heroine… slow down, learn to listen, and become an observer, and see yourself as the source of change within your own world.***

## Journaling and Notes

*The Second Moon Phase* - ***Rowan Moon - Wisdom Keeper***

## Desires, Goals, and Intentions, for the Coming Month

## Moon Dates March into April

- New Moon in Pisces – March 10
- First Quarter Moon in Cancer – March 17
- Spring Equinox Northern Hemisphere – Autumn Equinox Southern Hemisphere – March 20
- Full Moon Lunar Eclipse in Libra – March 25
- Last Quarter Moon in Capricorn – Aril 2

## The Third Moon Phase of 2024

### March 2024 / April 2024

### The Tree Lore of Ash and the Third Moon Weighs the Truth

***We are Each Responsible for the Consequences of Our Actions... Celebrate Your Conscious Choice and Free Will!***

As we move into March, the values and learning that underpin our personal growth and influence our creative manifestations come from the wisdom of Weighs the Truth aligning with the energy of Ash. In Tree Lore Ash is seen as being linked to the collective consciousness of humanity as a whole. Here in the UK, a couple of years before the covid pandemic, these trees fell prey to a virus, known as 'Ash Die Back' and in some circles this was seen as a mirror of what was about to take place in our human population.

In this Moon month, the energy of the Equinox signals a time of equal day and night, calling us to value the shadows as well as the light... it is often in passing through the darkness that we discover our greatest learning, and the influence of Weighs the Truth aligns with this flow of energy beautifully.

In this Moon time situations showed up in my world that required me to stand strong and to observe with compassion, whilst looking more deeply and asking why? To find answers, we need to ask questions. Why do we do what we do and what drives us to act in ways that are unhelpful or damaging to ourselves or to others? Weighs the Truth invites us to learn to evaluate circumstances in the here and now with compassion, and to take the time to build our awareness of all that has contributed to the current situation before deciding how best to respond, and the wisdom of the Ash Tree honors this... like a torch bearer, these trees reach tall and straight, holding the light and calling for the truth to be seen and heard.

Building on the lessons of the previous Lunar cycle and having made a conscious choice to process the past and see ourselves as the source of change in our lives in this Moon we learn to make this real by accepting full responsibility for the consequences of our actions. As humanity recovers and hopefully learns the lessons that come from such challenging times I am delighted to say that we are simultaneously seeing recovery and new growth appearing in our Ash forests. Yea!

Let's not forget that there is a vast amount of work to be done... and we each have our part to play... but if the Ash trees are truly a mirror of our collective consciousness then recovery and new growth is on the way... slowly but surely.

**Labradorite.**
**Aligning with the Third Moon Phase Weighs the Truth.**
**A pivotal month of transformation.**

Labradorite is known as a Stone of Transformation and is said to bring the wearer strength and perseverance, its energy heightening Spiritual connections whilst grounding and strengthening trust in both ourselves and the Universe. It is known as a 'revealer' in that it shows us the Truth behind the illusion and so cuts through the concepts of our limited ego mind.

I find this stone aids and enhances my creativity helping to bring focus and channel energy into conscious, direct actions of manifestation.

***We are Each Responsible for the Consequences of Our Actions...***
***Celebrate Your Conscious Choice and Free Will!***

## The New Moon – March 10th - 20° 16' Pisces

Piscean energy is highly spiritual and also very very emotional, so don't be surprised if during this Moon time you feel a heightened connectivity with divine assistance with increased intuition and greater psychic awareness.

Given that a New Moon is always a time of new beginnings and an opportunity to reset, the Pisces influence today will naturally invite you to enter a space of the dreamtime, and with your increased emotional and psychic sensitivity, find inspiration to formulate wishes that support creativity, imagination, and any aspects of your spiritual pathway.
If your wishes today include career choices, then make the most of the Piscean energy and craft wishes to support you in finding or creating a career pathway that will bring deep emotional fulfillment and align you with your spiritual and psychic gifts.
If you are wishing to meet a Soul mate or take an existing relationship to a whole other level of connection, or you have been previously hurt in love and relationship, this New Moon is perfect to wish for a relationship, that honors your spiritual journey, holds a deep soul connection, and establishes lasting trust through shared levels of emotional intelligence.
If you have been experiencing any difficulties around procrastination, perseverance, or any aspect of self-sabotage, that stems from any inner emotional turbulence, this is an amazing New Moon to make a personal commitment to yourself to let go of any self-defeating thinking patterns and behaviors and to ask for help to shift beyond these limitations. To align with the New Moon energy at its most powerful, be sure to write your wishes down during the 8 hours following the exact time of the New Moon in your location.

**New Moon Global Timings:**

- Los Angeles, USA — Sun, 10 Mar 2024 at 01:00 PST
- New York, USA — Sun, 10 Mar 2024 at 05:00 EDT
- Reykjavik, Iceland — Sun, 10 Mar 2024 at 09:00 GMT
- London, UK — Sun, 10 Mar 2024 at 09:00 GMT
- Paris, France — Sun, 10 Mar 2024 at 10:00 CET
- Cape Town, South Africa — Sun, 10 Mar 2024 at 11:00 SAST
- Delhi, India — Sun, 10 Mar 2024 at 14:30 IST
- Perth, Australia — Sun, 10 Mar 2024 at 17:00 AWST
- Tokyo, Japan — Sun, 10 Mar 2024 at 18:00 JST
- Sydney, Australia — Sun, 10 Mar 2024 at 20:00 AEDT
- Auckland, New Zealand — Sun, 10 Mar 2024 at 22:00 NZDT
- Greenwich Mean Time — Sun, 10 Mar 2024 at 09:00 GMT

## My Ten New Moon Wishes

*The Third Moon Phase – Ash Moon – Weighs the Truth*
*My Wishes and Dreams*

1

2

3

4

5

6

7

8

9

10

## My Ten New Moon Intentions

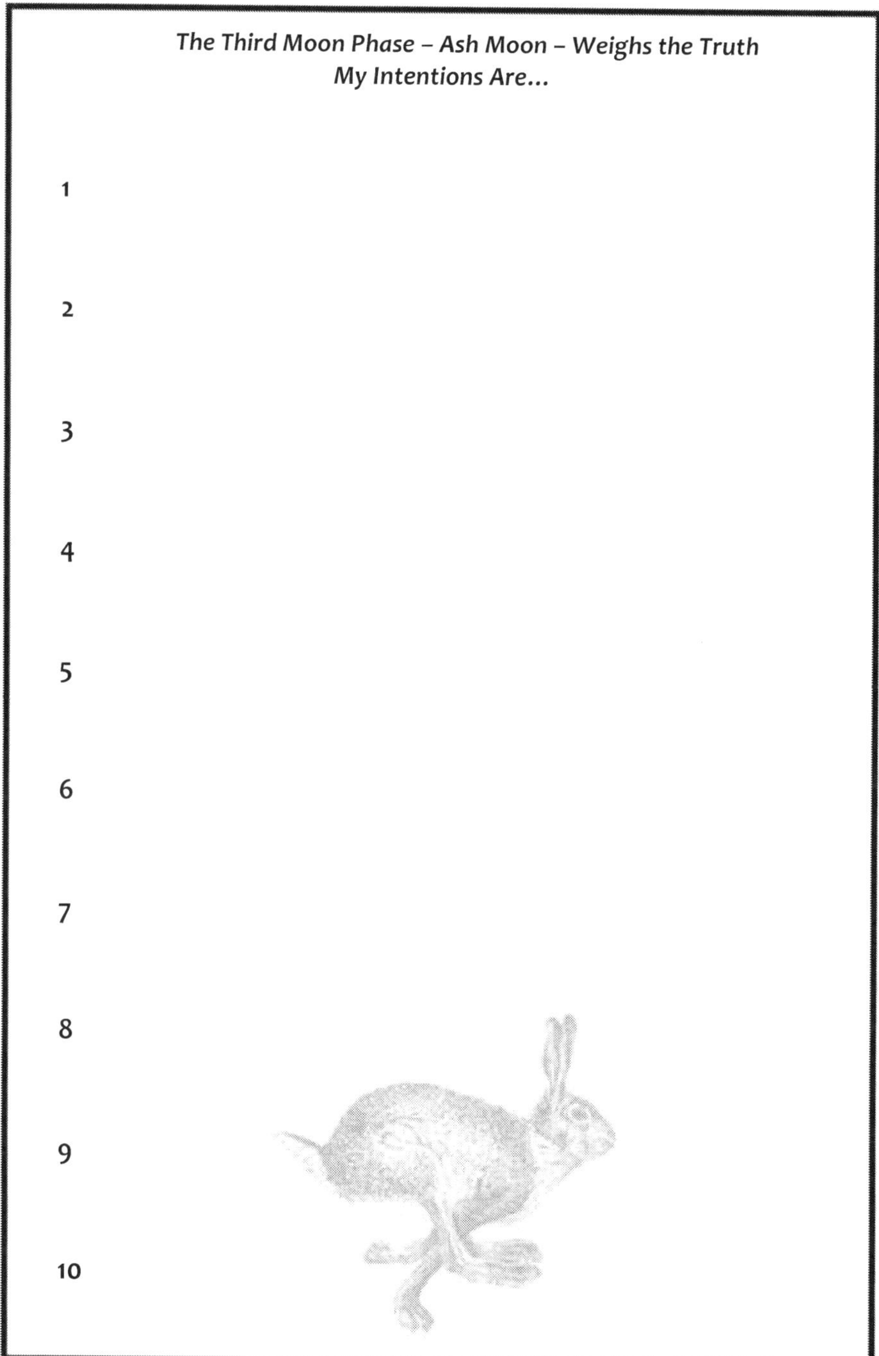

*The Third Moon Phase – Ash Moon – Weighs the Truth*
*My Intentions Are…*

1

2

3

4

5

6

7

8

9

10

## Journaling and Notes

***In Tree Lore Ash is seen as being linked to the collective consciousness of humanity as a whole acting as a mirror that highlights our overall health and wellbeing.***

## My First Quarter Moon Thoughts and Reviews

### The First Quarter Moon – March 17th - Cancer

*The energy of the Moon is now building and gathering momentum... we see her getting bigger and bigger by the day, so this is a great time to consider how and where you intend to channel and invest this growing expanding energy.*

*Look at where you are in your manifestations and your personal learning. What is showing up in your world right now? What is calling for your attention, and what do you need to prioritize? Where should you apply your greatest focus?*

## The Full Moon Lunar Eclipse – March 25th - 5° 07' Libra

Welcome to Eclipse season! A Full Moon in Libra will always be asking for balance, illuminating all aspects of your world that are working harmoniously… as well as any areas that are not, and as Libra is ruled by Venus, the planet of love, this energy often places a focus on relationships… and that will include your relationship with yourself. And the added weight of the Eclipse energy will turbo-charge these dynamics.

Any circumstances or situations that have been suppressed or denied may well surface or come to a head at this time, and you may find themes showing up that highlight insecurities and vulnerabilities, particularly in intimacy and the balance of giving and receiving in your relationships. And don't be phased if your buttons get pressed and some old wounds surface that haven't really healed properly… this is all showing up with purpose! Transformation is the name of the game today… with healing and rebalance being called for… both inner and outer.

You may also find that situations you have been investing in and manifesting may also come to a head, either in their completion or at a particular stage of their development, ready for the next phase and chapter to begin.

Each month place some rainwater or spring water in a bowl and leave it out overnight to absorb the energy of the Full Moon. Do NOT use a plastic bowl! Use glass or earthenware or any container whose fundamental ingredients come from a natural source. Collect the water afterwards and store it in a jar. Use the Moon Water in any of your ceremonies that support you to call in love, find equality and fairness in relationships, and any form of healing that helps with balance and the realignment of your energy flow and Chakras.

**Full Moon Global Timings:**

- Los Angeles, USA Mon, 25 Mar 2024 at 00:00 PDT
- New York, USA Mon, 25 Mar 2024 at 03:00 EDT
- Reykjavik, Iceland Mon, 25 Mar 2024 at 07:00 GMT
- London, UK Mon, 25 Mar 2024 at 07:00 GMT
- Paris, France Mon, 25 Mar 2024 at 08:00 CET
- Cape Town, South Africa Mon, 25 Mar 2024 at 09:00 SAST
- Delhi, India Mon, 25 Mar 2024 at 12:30 IST
- Perth, Australia Mon, 25 Mar 2024 at 15:00 AWST
- Tokyo, Japan Mon, 25 Mar 2024 at 16:00 JST
- Sydney, Australia Mon, 25 Mar 2024 at 18:00 AEDT
- Auckland, New Zealand Mon, 25 Mar 2024 at 20:00 NZDT
- Greenwich Mean Time Mon, 25 Mar 2024 at 07:00 GMT

## My Full Moon Insights and Illuminations

*The Third Moon Phase – Ash Moon – Weighs the Truth*

## Journaling and Notes

***Like a torch bearer, Ash trees reach tall and straight, holding the light and calling for the truth to be seen and heard.***

## My Last Quarter Moon Thoughts and Evaluations

### The Last Quarter Moon – April 2nd – Capricorn

*The Last Quarter Moon invites you to consolidate your progress and evaluate. Are any unwanted patterns still repeating? Are your plans, actions, and decisions congruent with all that you wish to be and all that you wish to see in the world?*

*The last quarter Moon marks a turning point and a shift in momentum. This is a magnificent time to journal in anticipation of setting clear and deeply personal New Moon wishes and intentions.*

## Journaling and Notes

*The energy of the Equinox signals a time of equal day and night, calling us to value the shadows as well as the light… it is often in passing through the darkness that we discover our greatest learning.*

## Journaling and Notes

*The Third Moon Phase – Ash Moon – Weighs the Truth*

## Desires, Goals, and Intentions, for the Coming Month

## Moon Dates April into May

- New Moon Solar Eclipse in Aries – April 8/9
- First Quarter Moon in Cancer – April 15
- Full Moon in Scorpio – April 23/24
- Last Quarter Moon in Aquarius – May 1
- Beltane Northern Hemisphere – Samhain Southern Hemisphere – May 1
- New Moon in Taurus - May 7/8

## The Fourth Moon Phase of 2024

### April 2024 / May 2024

### The Tree Lore of Alder and the Fourth Moon Looks Far Woman

***Observe with every sense that you have and with all that you are... this is a time to renew faith, trust, and love.***

In this Moon month our personal growth comes from the teachings of the Clan Mother, Looks Far Woman supported by the energy of Alder.

Sometimes known as the Goddess tree, the Tree Lore of Alder is steeped in myths and legends, all associated with finding the strength, determination, and the confidence needed to overcoming challenges, and develop discernment, resilience, and to pioneer new ways of seeing things. Alder is a tree whose life span is similar to our own and so this resilient tree doesn't waste a minute, and lives to the fullest.

Looks Far Woman is a seer and visionary, and when I first started exploring the Tribal Moon phases and really listening to myself and the way I was thinking and feeling, I noticed a very distinct shift in the energy between the Moon time of Weighs the Truth and Looks Far Woman. For me this Moon phase brought a new flow of energy that supported transition and urged in new possibilities. It coincides with the turning point of Beltane in the northern hemisphere and Samhain in the southern hemisphere, both of which are associated with a shift in energy and new beginnings.

During this Moon phase I found myself dreaming prolifically and a ton of signs, signals, and synchronicities were constantly showing up that tested my ability to trust my own real experiences and learn to recognize and believe in the guidance I was being shown. Balancing the ability to look the future with the importance of being fully present and grounded in the now, the story of Looks Far Woman alongside my real life happenings encouraged and inspired me to believe in possibility.

In terms of manifestation this is a powerful month. Following the growth of the third Moon phase where we learned to look beyond the obvious and gain understanding of cause and effect, this new phase of Lunar influence opens doorways of spiritual illumination that establish and renew faith, trust, and love.

**Angelite.**
**Aligning with the Fourth Moon Phase Looks Far Woman.**
**Trust, faith, and connection with the divine.**

Angelite is an extremely high vibrational stone that just emanates peace and tranquility. Attuning us to a higher frequency it is said to create a direct channel of communication with our guardian angels and has been known to initiate and stimulate the emergence of psychic gifts and mediumship.

It is also used in healing to facilitate the rebirthing process by opening the way for spiritual inspiration, creating opportunity for psychic channeling that links us with a higher vision and a greater universal consciousness.

***Observe with every sense that you have and with all that you are… this is a time to renew faith, trust, and love.***

# The New Moon Solar Eclipse – April 8th / 9th - 19° 23’ Aries

Eclipses are associated with your Karmic journey and are said to create an energetic rift or portal that can assist you to bring restoration to past issues, generate creative opportunities in the present, and with a vision of your future, connect you with your purpose and calling for this present lifetime.

So this is a time of transition and moving forwards with renewed energy and vitality and an Aries New Moon brings the focus on yourself, supporting personal growth, self-discovery, courage and authenticity, and independence. Aries energy is also very passionate so with things that are already moving along nicely you may feel incredibly motivated, but in areas of your world that are feeling slower or not quite ready to emerge yet, this energy could feel a bit more challenging.

If you struggle with indecisiveness or need to develop your assertiveness this is a great time to create focused wishes that ask for these issues to be easily addressed alongside clear intentions that commit you to following through with actions that move you forwards in real terms. The energy of Aries also supports new beginnings, so this is an excellent day to make targeted wishes that focus not only on your longer-term goals but also on those aspects of your plans that need focused attention and action right here and right now.

To engage with the New Moon energy at its most powerful, be sure to set your wishes and intentions during the 8 hours following the exact time of the New Moon in your location. Write them down and then open yourself to receive the guidance that you need to highlight the next steps on your pathway of manifestation.

**New Moon Global Timings:**

- Los Angeles, USA — Mon, 8 Apr 2024 at 11:20 PDT
- New York, USA — Mon, 8 Apr 2024 at 14:20 EDT
- Reykjavik, Iceland — Mon, 8 Apr 2024 at 18:20 GMT
- London, UK — Mon, 8 Apr 2024 at 19:20 BST
- Paris, France — Mon, 8 Apr 2024 at 20:20 CEST
- Cape Town, South Africa — Mon, 8 Apr 2024 at 20:20 SAST
- Delhi, India — Mon, 8 Apr 2024 at 23:50 IST
- Perth, Australia — Tue, 9 Apr 2024 at 02:20 AWST
- Tokyo, Japan — Tue, 9 Apr 2024 at 03:20 JST
- Sydney, Australia — Tue, 9 Apr 2024 at 04:20 AEST
- Auckland, New Zealand — Tue, 9 Apr 2024 at 06:20 NZST
- Greenwich Mean Time — Mon, 8 Apr 2024 at 18:20 GMT

## My Ten New Moon Wishes

*The Fourth Moon Phase - Alder Moon - Looks Far Woman*
*My Wishes and Dreams*

1

2

3

4

5

6

7

8

9

10

## My Ten New Moon Intentions

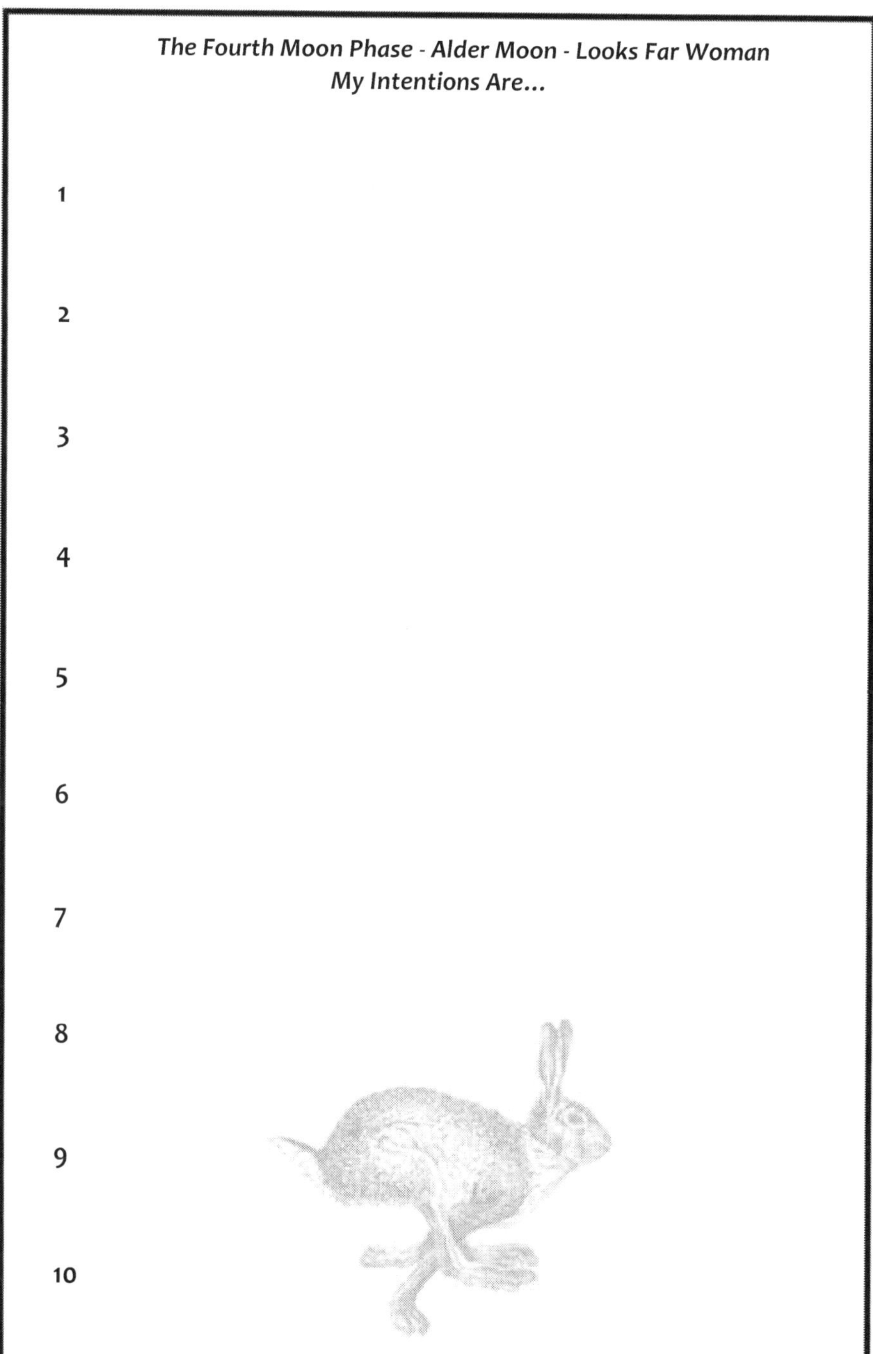

*The Fourth Moon Phase - Alder Moon - Looks Far Woman*
*My Intentions Are...*

1

2

3

4

5

6

7

8

9

10

## Journaling and Notes

***The Tree Lore of Alder is steeped in myths and legends, all associated with strength, determination, and the confidence to overcome challenges.***

## My First Quarter Moon Thoughts and Reviews

### The First Quarter Moon – April 15th - Cancer

*The energy of the Moon is now building and gathering momentum… we see her getting bigger and bigger by the day, so this is a great time to consider how and where you intend to channel and invest this growing expanding energy.*

*Look at where you are in your manifestations and your personal learning. What is showing up in your world right now? What is calling for your attention, and what do you need to prioritize? Where should you apply your greatest focus?*

## The Full Moon – April 23rd / 24th - 4° 17' Scorpio

The Full Moon in Scorpio invites you to deep dive into a space of profound awareness, peeling back the layers to help you to learn how to listen to yourself… and not simply listening with your ears… but listening with every sense that you have and all that you are. And with the added influence of Eclipse season, much may be revealed to you at this time which will ultimately be creating the opportunity to make informed choices.

So during this Moon time, hold a balanced perspective, be present and practice mindfulness, and let your experiences point the way. Become an observer and notice what is taking place around you and how this affects you. A Full Moon in Scorpio will tend to illuminate the shadows, inviting you to look at yourself and your life circumstances with truth and honesty. As the saying goes, when in deep water, become a diver! The Scorpio energy supports transformation and the letting go of things that no longer serve you, making room for renewal, and rebirth. If you are in anyway unsure of your calling or are seeking illumination and guidance to inform your pathway at this time then this powerful Full Moon is an ideal time to dedicate structured periods of meditate or to engage in Shamanic journeying. And if you find yourself dreaming prolifically, keep a dream journal as much may be revealed through this amazing avenue of communication with your unconscious.

Each month place some rainwater or spring water in a bowl and leave it out overnight to absorb the energy of the Full Moon. Do NOT use a plastic bowl! Use glass or earthenware or any container whose fundamental ingredients come from a natural source. Collect the water afterwards and store it in a jar. Use the Moon Water in any of your ceremonies that invite deep enquiry, transformation, and re-birth.

**Full Moon Global Timings:**

- Los Angeles, USA — Tue, 23 Apr 2024 at 16:48 PDT
- New York, USA — Tue, 23 Apr 2024 at 19:48 EDT
- Reykjavik, Iceland — Tue, 23 Apr 2024 at 23:48 GMT
- London, UK — Wed, 24 Apr 2024 at 00:48 BST
- Paris, France — Wed, 24 Apr 2024 at 01:48 CEST
- Cape Town, South Africa — Wed, 24 Apr 2024 at 01:48 SAST
- Delhi, India — Wed, 24 Apr 2024 at 05:18 IST
- Perth, Australia — Wed, 24 Apr 2024 at 07:48 AWST
- Tokyo, Japan — Wed, 24 Apr 2024 at 08:48 JST
- Sydney, Australia — Wed, 24 Apr 2024 at 09:48 AEST
- Auckland, New Zealand — Wed, 24 Apr 2024 at 11:48 NZST
- Greenwich Mean Time — Tue, 23 Apr 2024 at 23:48 GMT

## My Full Moon Insights and Illuminations

*The Fourth Moon Phase - Alder Moon - Looks Far Woman*

## Journaling and Notes

***This new phase of Lunar influence opens doorways of spiritual illumination that establish and renew faith, trust, and love.***

## My Last Quarter Moon Thoughts and Evaluations

### The Last Quarter Moon – May 1st – Aquarius

*The Last Quarter Moon invites you to consolidate your progress and evaluate. Are any unwanted patterns still repeating? Are your plans, actions, and decisions congruent with all that you wish to be and all that you wish to see in the world?*

*The last quarter Moon marks a turning point and a shift in momentum. This is a magnificent time to journal in anticipation of setting clear and deeply personal New Moon wishes and intentions.*

## Journaling and Notes

***The turning point of Beltane in the northern hemisphere and Samhain in the southern hemisphere, are associated with a shift in energy and new beginnings.***

## Journaling and Notes

*The Fourth Moon Phase - Alder Moon - Looks Far Woman*

## Desires, Goals, and Intentions, for the Coming Month

## Moon Dates May into June

- New Moon in Taurus - May 7/8
- First Quarter Moon in Leo - May 15
- Full Moon in Sagittarius – May 23/24
- Last Quarter Moon in Pisces – May 30
- New Moon in Gemini – June 6/7

# The Fifth Moon Phase of 2024

## May 2024 / June 2024

## The Tree Lore of Willow and the Fifth Moon Listening Woman

***Pay attention to what is said... and to what is not! When you listen to your heart you will always find the truth.***

This Moon phase is overseen by the Tree Lore of Willow connecting us with our deepest emotions and the teachings of Listening Woman. Willows thrive by water and beneath the surface their roots spread further and wider than any other tree, searching and seeking out the water under the ground. In the same way, as a therapist, I can assure you that your emotions are deeply intertwined with all that sits beneath the surface within you and in the landscape of your unconscious world. Willow is also a tree of love, whose influence asks you to both listen and speak from the heart.

During the Moon time of Listening Woman the circumstances that were showing up in my life required me to focus on the details of thoughts and words, both my own and those of others... and most importantly, the emotional content of the language.

Words carry power, a charismatic speaker can inspire an audience to be the very best version of themselves... or equally fuel them into behaving appallingly... and the power sits not simply in the message that's being said, but in the emotional content.

The life lessons that showed up for me during this Moon time helped me to listen through a different lens and to step back and from the drama within words that our ego mind can so easily create and buy into... and I listened carefully to what was being said through the emotional content of the words. The emotions within words will always speak of the actual intent... the underlying emotions will tell you if someone means something or not!

I also learned to really pick up on what was NOT being said! The absence of information in a conversation will tell you a lot about what is actually going on regardless of what is being presented. Likewise, when someone says something, but their actions tell a different story, it is wise to take note of this.

The learning of this Moon phase revolutionized my ability to develop healthy discernment and through well informed listening with recognition and ownership of my personal choices and responses I started to manage and maintain my boundaries with strength and confidence.

## Agate Blue Lace.
## Aligning with the Fifth Moon Phase Listening Woman.
## Look beyond the obvious, there is a story to be heard.

Said to improve concentration, perception, and mental sharpness the powerfully transformative energy of Agate eliminates and transforms negativity, energizing a sense of safety and security through the holding of firm boundaries.

Cleansing us from the inside out and reaching into our Aura, Blue Lace Agate not only carries all of the fundamental qualities of Agate but seems to add an additional energy of peace and tranquility. Said to sooth the voice and release any restrictive energy around the throat Chakra, this powerful little stone supports us in finding a voice to express thoughts and feelings with a calm and mindful clarity.

***Pay attention to what is said... and to what is not! When you listen with your heart you will always find the truth.***

## The New Moon – May 7th / 8th - 18° 01' Taurus

A Taurus Moon will naturally place an emphasis on security and stability and earthy things, like health, your physical body, possessions, and money, as well as personal qualities such as patience, perseverance, confidence, and self-worth. So this New Moon is an amazing time to make wishes around home, family, finances, and all aspects of health including the health of your self-esteem and emotional wellness. Use this New Moon to make wishes to help you to remove any blocks in these areas of your life and bring you the energy and commitment that you need to overcome self-doubt and let go of any insecurities or unhelpful habits that have previously held you back and stopped you from progressing.
If you struggle with pacing yourself effectively and find that your energy levels swing from being slow and sluggish to charging ahead without any brakes, or your mindset and emotions swing from being ultra-positive to ultra-negative, then use this Moon to make wishes that support a more balanced and consistent approach.
If you are someone who struggles with impatience, and you get a little bit impulsive then set wishes that harness the Taurus energy, and rather than being a bull in a china shop, support you in making consistent, steady progress and to persevere. This is also a particularly good Moon time to focus on the differences between wishes and intentions. The combination of the two brings a balanced energy that supports you to commit fully to a new pro-active approach that will take you out of your safe zone and into your stretch zone, building your confidence slowly and steadily.

To engage with the New Moon energy at its most powerful, be sure to write your wishes down during the 8 hours following the exact time of the New Moon in your location.

**New Moon Global Timings:**

- Los Angeles, USA — Tue, 7 May 2024 at 20:21 PDT
- New York, USA — Tue, 7 May 2024 at 23:21 EDT
- Reykjavik, Iceland — Wed, 8 May 2024 at 03:21 GMT
- London, UK — Wed, 8 May 2024 at 04:21 BST
- Paris, France — Wed, 8 May 2024 at 05:21 CEST
- Cape Town, South Africa — Wed, 8 May 2024 at 05:21 SAST
- Delhi, India — Wed, 8 May 2024 at 08:51 IST
- Perth, Australia — Wed, 8 May 2024 at 11:21 AWST
- Tokyo, Japan — Wed, 8 May 2024 at 12:21 JST
- Sydney, Australia — Wed, 8 May 2024 at 13:21 AEST
- Auckland, New Zealand — Wed, 8 May 2024 at 15:21 NZST
- Greenwich Mean Time — Wed, 8 May 2024 at 03:21 GMT

## My Ten New Moon Wishes

*The Fifth Moon Phase - Willow Moon - Listening Woman*
*My Wishes and Dreams*

1

2

3

4

5

6

7

8

9

10

## My Ten New Moon Intentions

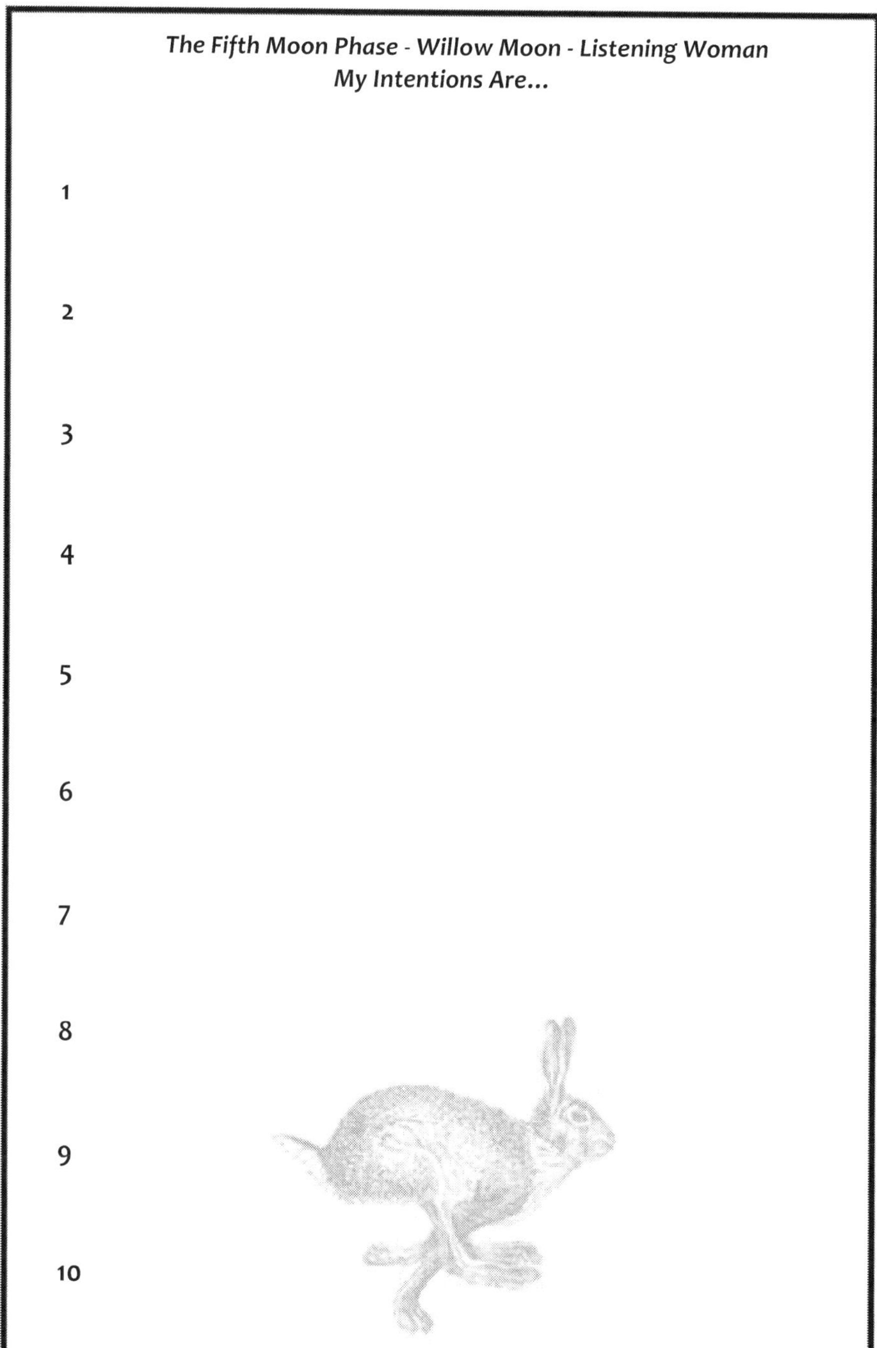

*The Fifth Moon Phase - Willow Moon - Listening Woman*
*My Intentions Are...*

1

2

3

4

5

6

7

8

9

10

## Journaling and Notes

*Your emotions are deeply intertwined with all that sits beneath the surface within you and in the landscape of your unconscious world.*

## My First Quarter Moon Thoughts and Reviews

### The First Quarter Moon – May 15th – Leo

*The energy of the Moon is now building and gathering momentum... we see her getting bigger and bigger by the day, so this is a great time to consider how and where you intend to channel and invest this growing expanding energy.*

*Look at where you are in your manifestations and your personal learning. What is showing up in your world right now? What is calling for your attention, and what do you need to prioritize? Where should you apply your greatest focus?*

## The Full Moon – May 23rd / 24th - 4° 17' Sagittarius

A Full Moon in Sagittarius is primed to illuminate any areas of your world that are striving for change, and through embracing an attitude of gratitude, open avenues of hope and optimism that set the pace for the future. This is a Moon time that calls for completions and potential healing with the Sagittarian influence inviting you to free yourself from anything that holds you back, requesting that you tie up loose ends and begin to formulate and plan for the next phase on your journey of manifestation.

To make the very best of this energy flow, pause, get still, and observe the timeline of your life, reflecting on your past, your present and your future, the interconnectedness of events, and your own point of power in the here and now, and align yourself with the empowerment that this awareness brings. This Moon time may also highlight the connection between your thoughts and your words and your external reality, bringing opportunity to observe these connections, and then make conscious changes to any internal blocks of negativity that could be hindering your ongoing manifestations. Lean into this space of awareness and potential with passion and vigor. This Moon will want to connect you with renewed enthusiasm, and ignite your passions, especially in areas of life that connect with justice, purpose, and freedom, clearing the way for new optimism.

Each month place some rainwater or spring water in a bowl and leave it out overnight to absorb the energy of the Full Moon. Do NOT use a plastic bowl! Use glass or earthenware or any container whose fundamental ingredients come from a natural source. Collect the water afterwards and store it in a jar. Use this Moon Water in any of your ceremonies that support the letting go of inhibitions and negative thinking patterns, bring healing for depression, support freedom, justice, and equality, and align you with hope and optimism.

**Full Moon Global Timings:**

- Los Angeles, USA — Thu, 23 May 2024 at 06:52 PDT
- New York, USA — Thu, 23 May 2024 at 09:52 EDT
- Reykjavik, Iceland — Thu, 23 May 2024 at 13:52 GMT
- London, UK — Thu, 23 May 2024 at 14:52 BST
- Paris, France — Thu, 23 May 2024 at 15:52 CEST
- Cape Town, South Africa — Thu, 23 May 2024 at 15:52 SAST
- Delhi, India — Thu, 23 May 2024 at 19:22 IST
- Perth, Australia — Thu, 23 May 2024 at 21:52 AWST
- Tokyo, Japan — Thu, 23 May 2024 at 22:52 JST
- Sydney, Australia — Thu, 23 May 2024 at 23:52 AEST
- Auckland, New Zealand — Fri, 24 May 2024 at 01:52 NZST
- Greenwich Mean Time — Thu, 23 May 2024 at 13:52 GMT

## My Full Moon Insights and Illuminations

*The Fifth Moon Phase - Willow Moon - Listening Woman*

## Journaling and Notes

*Willow is a tree of love, whose influence asks you to listen through your heart and then speak from the heart.*

## My Last Quarter Moon Thoughts and Evaluations

### The Last Quarter Moon – May 30th – Pisces

*The Last Quarter Moon invites you to consolidate your progress and evaluate. Are any unwanted patterns still repeating? Are your plans, actions, and decisions congruent with all that you wish to be and all that you wish to see in the world?*

*The last quarter Moon marks a turning point and a shift in momentum. This is a magnificent time to journal in anticipation of setting clear and deeply personal New Moon wishes and intentions.*

## Journaling and Notes

*The learning of this Moon phase revolutionized my ability to develop healthy discernment and through well informed listening with recognition and ownership of my personal choices.*

## Journaling and Notes

*The Fifth Moon Phase - Willow Moon - Listening Woman*

## Desires, Goals, and Intentions, for the Coming Month

## Moon Dates June into July

- New Moon in Gemini - June 6/7
- First Quarter Moon in Virgo - June 14
- Summer Solstice Northern Hemisphere – Winter Solstice Southern Hemisphere – June 21
- Full Moon in Capricorn – June 21/22
- Last Quarter Moon in Aries – June 28
- New Moon in Cancer - July 5/6

## The Sixth Moon Phase of 2024

### June 2024 / July 2024

### The Tree Lore of Hawthorn and the Sixth Moon Storyteller

***What would you like to change in your world? It's time to re-write your own script... let your new story unfold!***

During this Lunar month the values and learning come from the Tree Lore of Hawthorn, whose energy aligns with protection, teaching us that personal strength stems from the recognition of our own power and the ability to take charge of this, without any need to exert power over others and the wisdom of Storyteller whose teachings bring much opportunity for heightened levels of awareness and the revealing of historic, auto-pilot patterns of behavior, with an opportunity to release and transform. I found this Moon time to be a magical month of significant shifts and subsequent empowerment... however, the stuff that shows up to get this process going may not always be easy.

During the Moon time of Storyteller, I found myself dreaming about and reflecting on my own history and I began to appreciate that everything that had happened in my life had formed and established who I have become and the values that I hold so dear. It also became very clear to me that whilst I have no control over the pathways of others, I can view their actions with compassion.

If I don't like someone's actions, it is empowering to remember that I do not know what brought them to this point in their journey, and if their actions are causing damage, then I can be almost certain that they are still carrying unresolved issues from their past... however, it is not my responsibility to fix them or try to direct them. Their choices are their own. Likewise, if I don't like any aspects of my own life or I am still living through any outdated assumptions, attitudes, or perspectives that are rooted in the past, then I can change this. Storyteller highlights the lessons that our life circumstances bring us and through awareness with compassion, invites us to grow beyond these limitations.

The lessons and qualities of Hawthorn support the insight of this month of growth and potential. These tress were once planted in thousands to create strong protective boundaries around homesteads, fields, and livestock enclosures, and can actually live for up to 700 years and so have been witness to many generations of our history, remaining generous and giving throughout. They are humble and yet magnificent, and above all resilient and protective, holding the wisdom of history and standing the test of time. It is said that if you spend time with a Hawthorn tree it will help you to let go of the conditioned thinking patterns that separate you from the natural world. A gift indeed.

**Lapis Lazuli.**
**Aligning with the Sixth Moon Phase Storyteller.**
**What is your story?**

Be the change that you wish to see in the world! Stand in your truth and find your voice! This magnificent stone radiates the energy of the Spiritual Warrior striving to walk a pathway of authenticity.

Lapis Lazuli is a powerful stone of self-expression. Said to reveal our inner truth through self-awareness, this extraordinary stone is said to encourage us to uphold honesty and integrity whilst observing ourselves and others through the eyes of compassion.

***What would you like to change in your world? It's time to re-write your own script… let your new story unfold!***

## The New Moon – June 6th / 7th - 16° 17’ Gemini

The Gemini Moon time brings a beautifully creative flow of energy that invites you to evaluate your options, weigh up every possibility and view all sides of the story before making informed choices and decisions. The Gemini influence naturally invites curiosity bringing exactly the inspiration you need to create change and find solutions through enquiry and discovery, supporting restructuring and progression with opportunity to course correct where needed.

A New Moon in Gemini lends itself beautifully to wishes and intentions that support better and fluent communication, clear thinking and speaking, and the calming of mental energy, so if you find yourself weighing up different avenues of potential possibilities use your New Moon wishes to ask for clarity as to the best option for you at this moment in time.

If you feel restless or uneasy, take this seriously and make time to listen to the source of these feelings.. have that conversation with yourself and take some time to internally unpack, then use your increased awareness to formulate your New Moon wishes and intentions with renewed clarity.

If you feel the need to have a voice today or to speak your truth or you need to find a clarity of thought or direction the energy of a Gemini New moon naturally invites curiosity and brings the inspiration we need to create change

In your New Moon ceremonies write down your 10 wishes and open yourself to receive the guidance that you need to highlight the next steps on your pathway of manifestation. To engage with the New Moon energy at its most powerful, be sure to write your wishes down during the 8 hours following the exact time of the New Moon in your location.

**New Moon Global Timings:**

- Los Angeles, USA Thu, 6 Jun 2024 at 05:37 PDT
- New York, USA Thu, 6 Jun 2024 at 08:37 EDT
- Reykjavik, Iceland Thu, 6 Jun 2024 at 12:37 GMT
- London, UK Thu, 6 Jun 2024 at 13:37 BST
- Paris, France Thu, 6 Jun 2024 at 14:37 CEST
- Cape Town, South Africa Thu, 6 Jun 2024 at 14:37 SAST
- Delhi, India Thu, 6 Jun 2024 at 18:07 IST
- Perth, Australia Thu, 6 Jun 2024 at 20:37 AWST
- Tokyo, Japan Thu, 6 Jun 2024 at 21:37 JST
- Sydney, Australia Thu, 6 Jun 2024 at 22:37 AEST
- Auckland, New Zealand Fri, 7 Jun 2024 at 00:37 NZST
- Greenwich Mean Time Thu, 6 Jun 2024 at 12:37 GMT

## My Ten New Moon Wishes

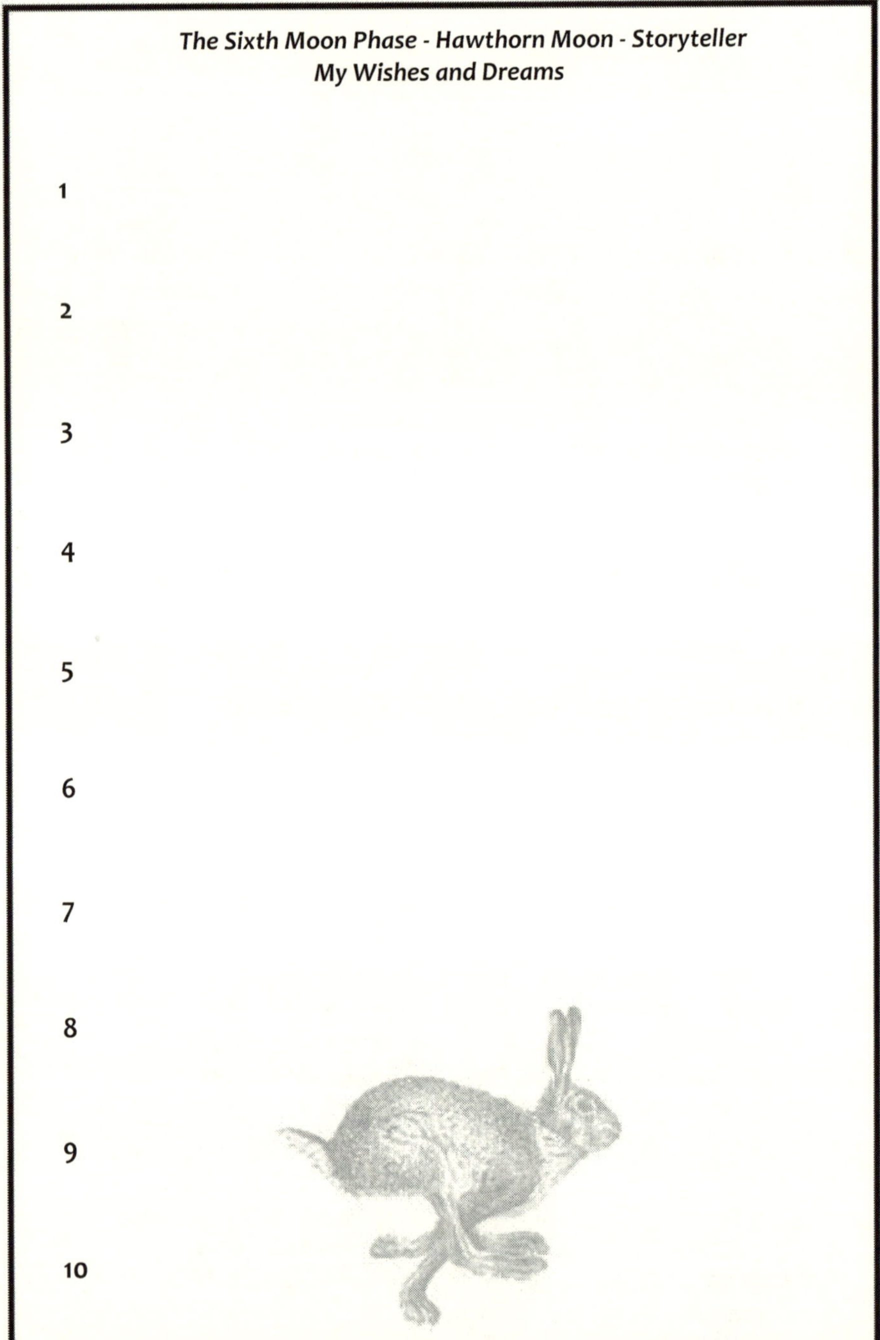

*The Sixth Moon Phase - Hawthorn Moon - Storyteller*
*My Wishes and Dreams*

1

2

3

4

5

6

7

8

9

10

## My Ten New Moon Intentions

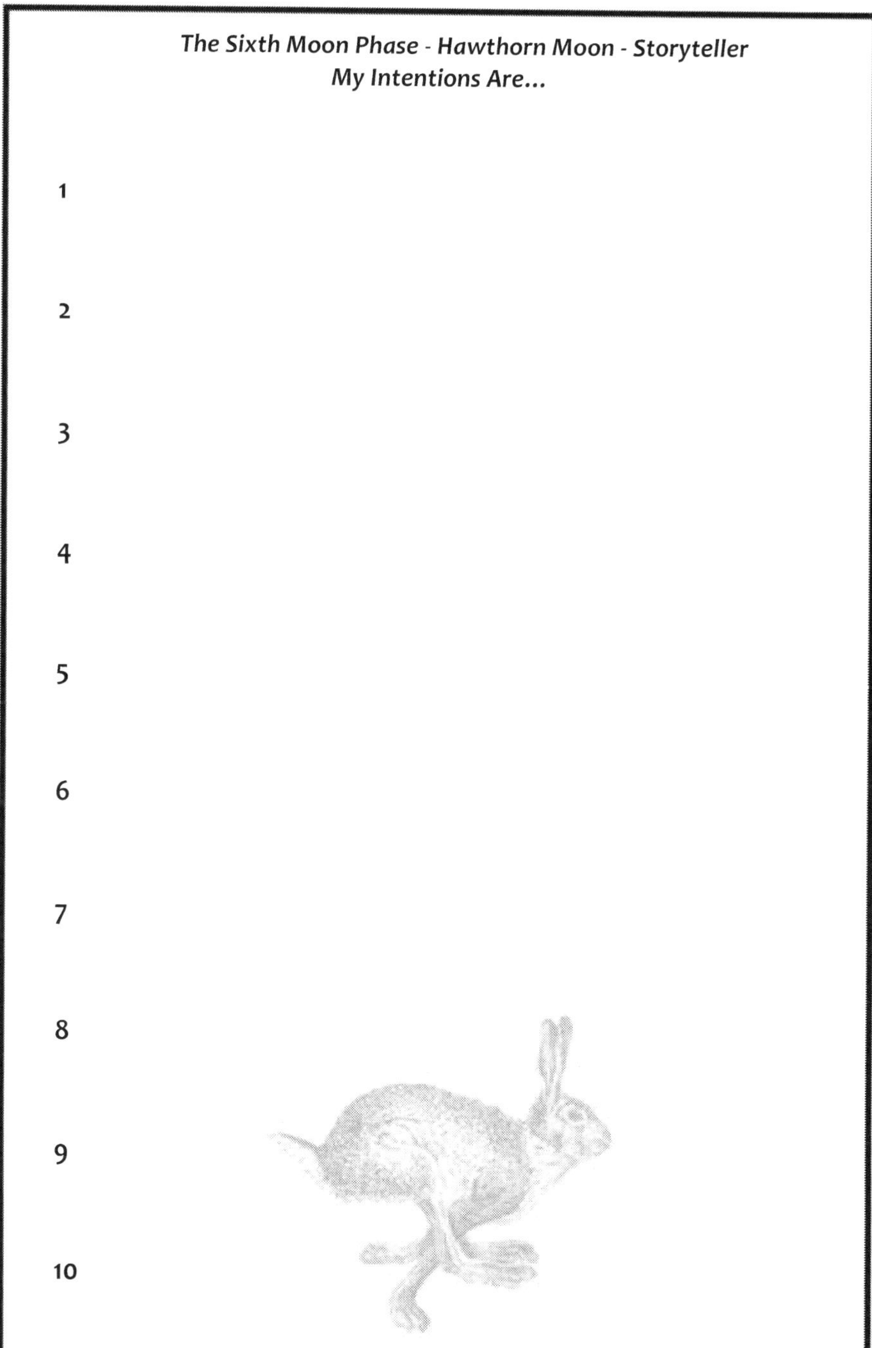

*The Sixth Moon Phase - Hawthorn Moon - Storyteller*
*My Intentions Are...*

1

2

3

4

5

6

7

8

9

10

## Journaling and Notes

***Storyteller highlights the lessons that our life circumstances bring us and through awareness with compassion, invites us to grow beyond these limitations.***

## My First Quarter Moon Thoughts and Reviews

### The First Quarter Moon – June 14th – Virgo

*The energy of the Moon is now building and gathering momentum... we see her getting bigger and bigger by the day, so this is a great time to consider how and where you intend to channel and invest this growing expanding energy.*

***Look at where you are in your manifestations and your personal learning. What is showing up in your world right now? What is calling for your attention, and what do you need to prioritize? Where should you apply your greatest focus?***

## The Full Moon – June 21st / 22nd - 1° 06' Capricorn

The Full Moon in steady solid earthy Capricorn asks you to get still, and to anchor yourself in the truth of your own real experiences, bringing opportunity for a very real and very honest review with a realistic summing up and appraisal.
We define our future goals not only from the experiences that we love, but also from the experiences in our lives that have presented us with challenge and difficulty. Capricorn is ruled by karmic Saturn, asking us to learn from experience and integrate this awareness into our growth with understanding and appreciation, i.e. learning from our mistakes as well as from our successes.

Given that a Capricorn Moon brings a natural focus to your ambitions, goals, and personal desires, both personal and professional, this Full Moon period may well illuminate any inner blocks to your success, such as self-doubt or a lack of confidence, and any self-sabotaging thinking patterns or behaviors. This Moon time may also highlight areas where you have overextended yourself or need to get more organized in terms of your timetabling and successful time management. The influence of a Capricorn Full Moon can also highlight pathways that align your ambitions with your true purpose and calling with pragmatic and practical steps to manifest this into being... so whatever shows up in your world at this time you can be sure that it is bringing valuable information and purpose.

Each month place some rainwater or spring water in a bowl and leave it out overnight to absorb the energy of the Full Moon. Do NOT use a plastic bowl! Use glass or earthenware or any container whose fundamental ingredients come from a natural source. Collect the water afterwards and store it in a jar. Use this Moon Water in any of your ceremonies that focus on Karmic progression and transformation and align your ambitions and desires with your true calling, purpose, and destiny.

**Full Moon Global Timings:**

- Los Angeles, USA — Fri, 21 Jun 2024 at 18:07 PDT
- New York, USA — Fri, 21 Jun 2024 at 21:07 EDT
- Reykjavik, Iceland — Sat, 22 Jun 2024 at 01:07 GMT
- London, UK — Sat, 22 Jun 2024 at 02:07 BST
- Paris, France — Sat, 22 Jun 2024 at 03:07 CEST
- Cape Town, South Africa — Sat, 22 Jun 2024 at 03:07 SAST
- Delhi, India — Sat, 22 Jun 2024 at 06:37 IST
- Perth, Australia — Sat, 22 Jun 2024 at 09:07 AWST
- Tokyo, Japan — Sat, 22 Jun 2024 at 10:07 JST
- Sydney, Australia — Sat, 22 Jun 2024 at 11:07 AEST
- Auckland, New Zealand — Sat, 22 Jun 2024 at 13:07 NZST
- Greenwich Mean Time — Sat, 22 Jun 2024 at 01:07 GMT

## My Full Moon Insights and Illuminations

*The Sixth Moon Phase - Hawthorn Moon - Storyteller*

## Journaling and Notes

***It is said that if you spend time with a Hawthorn tree it will help you to let go of the conditioned thinking patterns that separate you from the natural world……. A gift indeed.***

## My Last Quarter Moon Thoughts and Evaluations

### The Last Quarter Moon – June 28th – Aries

*The Last Quarter Moon invites you to consolidate your progress and evaluate. Are any unwanted patterns still repeating? Are your plans, actions, and decisions congruent with all that you wish to be and all that you wish to see in the world?*

*The last quarter Moon marks a turning point and a shift in momentum. This is a magnificent time to journal in anticipation of setting clear and deeply personal New Moon wishes and intentions.*

## Journaling and Notes

***Personal strength stems from the recognition of our own power and the ability to take charge of this, without any need to exert power over others.***

## Journaling and Notes

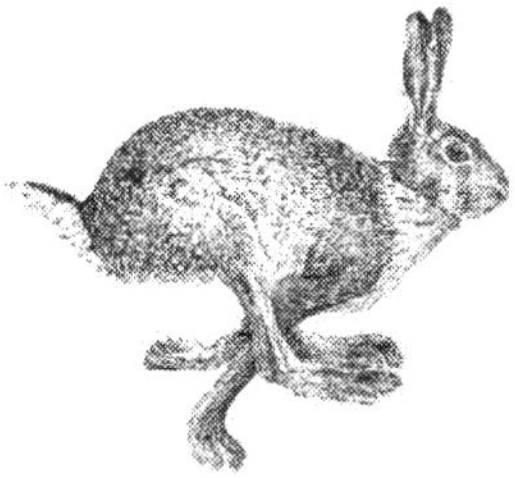

*The Sixth Moon Phase - Hawthorn Moon - Storyteller*

## Desires, Goals, and Intentions, for the Coming Month

## Moon Dates July into August

- New Moon in Cancer - July 5/6
- First Quarter Moon in Libra – July 13/14
- Full Moon in Capricorn – July 21
- Last Quarter Moon in Taurus - July 28
- Lammas Northern Hemisphere - Imbolc Southern Hemisphere – August 1
- New Moon in Leo – August 4

## The Seventh Moon Phase of 2024

### July 2024 / August 2024

### The Tree Lore of Oak and the Seventh Moon Loves All Things

***An intention is a statement that places the seeds of your personal visions into the garden of the Universe creating the future for generations to come.***

In this Moon month the teachings of Oak unite with the Clan Moon Mother, Loves All Things. Both speak to us about the circle of life and remind us to love and appreciate the present and value the abundance of all that we have in the immediacy of now, whilst recognizing that how we are living right now is impacting the wellbeing of future generations yet to come.

During this Moon time the events in my life perfectly mirrored so much of the learning of Loves All Things. When we are shrouded in our own emotions, particularly the challenging ones, it is easy to lose sight of the extraordinariness of everything that surrounds us. Hearing her story of love and loss, I was able to navigate a very close loss in my own life, without losing faith or trust in life, if anything, my appreciation of life, especially the really tiny things that can so easily go unnoticed, was massively enhanced and I was able to approach love and see love in a very different way.

The lessons of Oak highlight our relationship and interconnectedness with all of life, but especially the relationship between ourselves and the magnificent Tree beings of our planet. Oak is a tree that is steeped in historical connections with our human species and also one that in real terms actively helps to balance some of the environmental challenges that we as a collective humanity have created on this planet. Trees draw carbon from the atmosphere, which is then locked into their growth with some trees being more active in this than others. A 100 year old Oak tree will hold around 3 tons of carbon within its very structure doing us and our planet a marvelous service. Perhaps not surprisingly, rather like the crystal of amethyst, Oak is seen as a master healer and is also known as a witness tree. Traditionally many ceremonies were held beneath an Oak tree giving the intent of the ceremony a seal of approval.

For me, the Moon time of the magnificent Oak and Loves All Things offers us a return to Love in every aspect of our lives with a personal liberation that comes from this level of Soul growth. Through teachings that foster the best in ourselves and others through nurture and validation, and with acceptance and forgiveness of both ourselves and others we discover a much deeper sense of self-respect and therefore respect of others and of all of life.

## Moonstone.
## Aligning with the Seventh Moon Phase Loves All Things.
## Love Heals All.

Moonstone invites us to open our hearts and to love without judgment. It is associated with fertility and sensuality connecting us with the inner goddess that sits within us all, heightening our intuition, and clearing and cleansing our mind from any negative emotions, especially those connected to our relationships.

Used in meditation, particularly at the time of the New Moon, it is said to enhance our powers of manifestation. Moonstone brings a wonderful energy into any New Moon ceremonies associated with our dreams, wishes and desires reminding us of the Miracles that surround us and of the infinite support of Spirit and the Universe.

***An intention is a statement that places the seeds of your personal visions into the garden of the Universe creating the future for generations to come.***

## The New Moon – July 5$^{th}$ / 6$^{th}$ - 14° 23’ Cancer

The energy of a Cancer New Moon will naturally create a focus on your sense of belonging, your community, your home, and your family, with an emphasis on your own internal feelings and emotions about these areas of your life.

The influence of Cancer also emphasizes healing, nurture, and a balanced flow of energy, so the stuff in your world that is already in balance and in gentle flow will receive an even greater flow of support from wishes and intentions that invite reliable steady growth, with continued nurture and healing. However, if any of your buttons have been recently pressed and you’ve been feeling the need to retreat into your shell, then take a good look at where you need to heal and set wishes and intentions that support a program of self-care.

This is a Moon that invites you to nurture your dreams and surround your hopes for the future in love and care, and will naturally support transition through nurture, understanding, and kindness. If you are someone who feels particularly vulnerable during times of change and transition the energy of this New Moon will lend itself beautifully to wishes that release you from anxiety and insecurity, inviting stability and emotional strength and resilience. And if you have been hurt in the past, this is an ideal New Moon to set wishes to invite new and harmonious relationships into your life that maintain a healthy balance of giving and receiving.

In your New Moon ceremonies write down your 10 wishes and open yourself to receive the guidance that you need to highlight the next steps on your pathway of manifestation. To engage with the New Moon energy at its most powerful, be sure to write your wishes down during the 8 hours following the exact time of the New Moon in your location.

**New Moon Global Timings:**

- Los Angeles, USA — Fri, 5 Jul 2024 at 15:57 PDT
- New York, USA — Fri, 5 Jul 2024 at 18:57 EDT
- Reykjavik, Iceland — Fri, 5 Jul 2024 at 22:57 GMT
- London, UK — Fri, 5 Jul 2024 at 23:57 BST
- Paris, France — Sat, 6 Jul 2024 at 00:57 CEST
- Cape Town, South Africa — Sat, 6 Jul 2024 at 00:57 SAST
- Delhi, India — Sat, 6 Jul 2024 at 04:27 IST
- Perth, Australia — Sat, 6 Jul 2024 at 06:57 AWST
- Tokyo, Japan — Sat, 6 Jul 2024 at 07:57 JST
- Sydney, Australia — Sat, 6 Jul 2024 at 08:57 AEST
- Auckland, New Zealand — Sat, 6 Jul 2024 at 10:57 NZST
- Greenwich Mean Time — Fri, 5 Jul 2024 at 22:57 GMT

## My Ten New Moon Wishes

*The Seventh Moon Phase – Oak Moon – Loves All Things*
*My Wishes and Dreams*

1

2

3

4

5

6

7

8

9

10

# My Ten New Moon Intentions

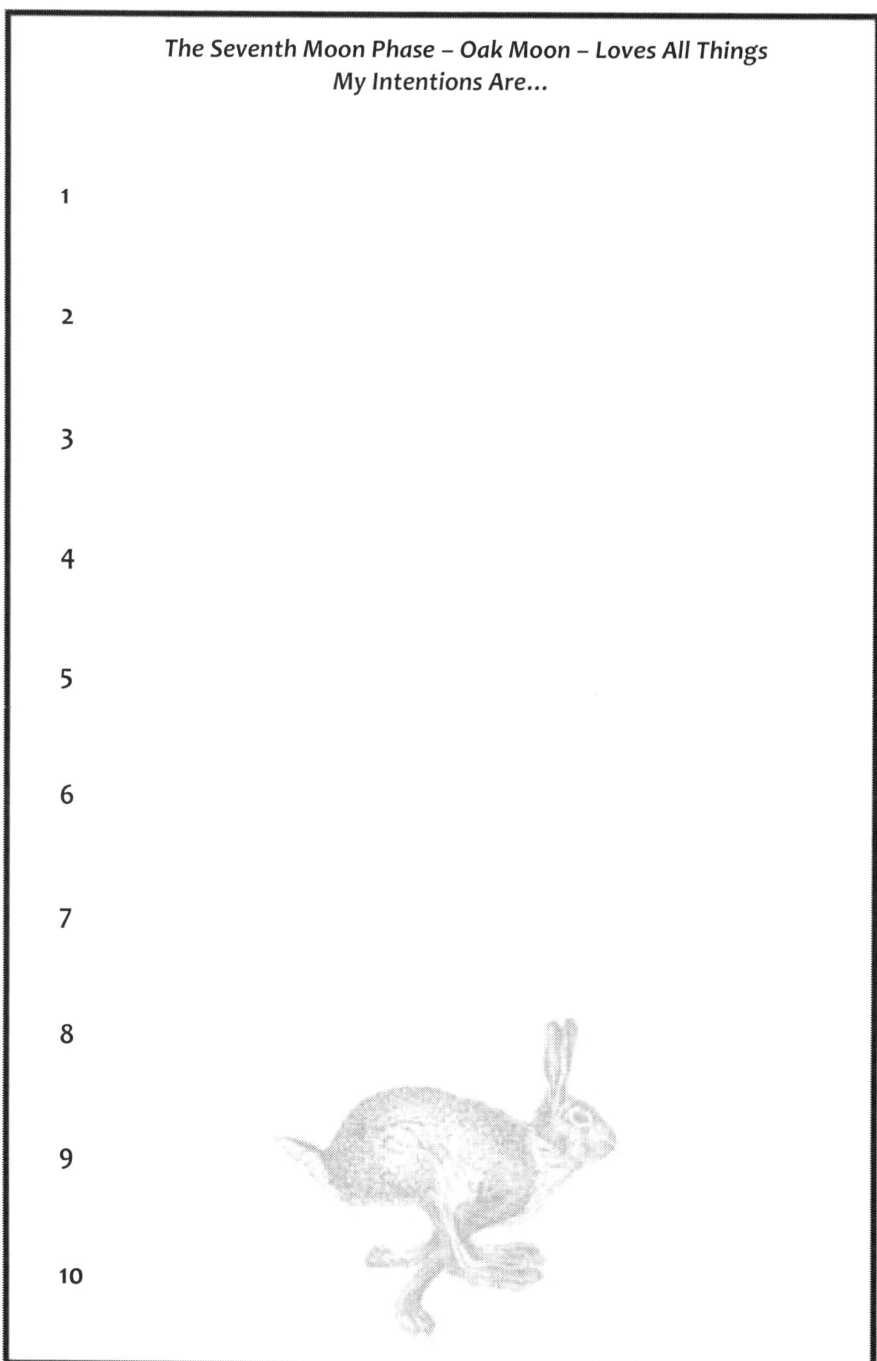

*The Seventh Moon Phase – Oak Moon – Loves All Things*
*My Intentions Are...*

1

2

3

4

5

6

7

8

9

10

## Journaling and Notes

*The way that we are each living right now is impacting the wellbeing of future generations yet to come.*

## My First Quarter Moon Thoughts and Reviews

### The First Quarter Moon – July 13th / 14th – Libra

*The energy of the Moon is now building and gathering momentum… we see her getting bigger and bigger by the day, so this is a great time to consider how and where you intend to channel and invest this growing expanding energy.*

*Look at where you are in your manifestations and your personal learning. What is showing up in your world right now? What is calling for your attention, and what do you need to prioritize? Where should you apply your greatest focus?*

## The Full Moon – July 21st - 29° 08' Capricorn

The Full Moon in steady solid earthy Capricorn asks you to get still, and to anchor yourself in the truth of your own real experiences, bringing opportunity for a very real and very honest review with a realistic summing up and appraisal.
We define our future goals not only from the experiences that we love, but also from the experiences in our lives that have presented us with challenge and difficulty. Capricorn is ruled by karmic Saturn, asking us to learn from experience and integrate this awareness into our growth with understanding and appreciation, i.e. learning from our mistakes as well as from our successes.
Given that a Capricorn Moon brings a natural focus to your ambitions, goals, and personal desires, both personal and professional, this Full Moon period may well illuminate any inner blocks to your success, such as self-doubt or a lack of confidence, and any self-sabotaging thinking patterns or behaviors.
This Moon time may also highlight areas where you have overextended yourself or need to get more organized in terms of your timetabling and successful time management.
The influence of a Capricorn Full Moon can also highlight pathways that align your ambitions with your true purpose and calling with pragmatic and practical steps to manifest this into being… so whatever shows up in your world at this time you can be sure that it is bringing valuable information and arriving with purpose.
Each month place some rainwater or spring water in a bowl and leave it out overnight to absorb the energy of the Full Moon. Do NOT use a plastic bowl! Use glass or earthenware or any container whose fundamental ingredients come from a natural source. Collect the water afterwards and store it in a jar.
Use this Moon Water in any of your ceremonies that focus on Karmic progression and transformation and align your ambitions and desires with your true calling, purpose, and destiny.

**Full Moon Global Timings:**

- Los Angeles, USA Sun, 21 Jul 2024 at 03:16 PDT
- New York, USA Sun, 21 Jul 2024 at 06:16 EDT
- Reykjavik, Iceland Sun, 21 Jul 2024 at 10:16 GMT
- London, UK Sun, 21 Jul 2024 at 11:16 BST
- Paris, France Sun, 21 Jul 2024 at 12:16 CEST
- Cape Town, South Africa Sun, 21 Jul 2024 at 12:16 SAST
- Delhi, India Sun, 21 Jul 2024 at 15:46 IST
- Perth, Australia Sun, 21 Jul 2024 at 18:16 AWST
- Tokyo, Japan Sun, 21 Jul 2024 at 19:16 JST
- Sydney, Australia Sun, 21 Jul 2024 at 20:16 AEST
- Auckland, New Zealand Sun, 21 Jul 2024 at 22:16 NZST
- Greenwich Mean Time Sun, 21 Jul 2024 at 10:16 GMT

## My Full Moon Insights and Illuminations

*The Seventh Moon Phase – Oak Moon – Loves All Things*

## Journaling and Notes

*A 100 year old Oak tree will hold around 3 tons of carbon within its very structure doing us and our planet a marvelous service.*

## My Last Quarter Moon Thoughts and Evaluations

### The Last Quarter Moon – July 28th – Taurus

*The Last Quarter Moon invites you to consolidate your progress and evaluate. Are any unwanted patterns still repeating? Are your plans, actions, and decisions congruent with all that you wish to be and all that you wish to see in the world?*

*The last quarter Moon marks a turning point and a shift in momentum. This is a magnificent time to journal in anticipation of setting clear and deeply personal New Moon wishes and intentions.*

## Journaling and Notes

*With acceptance and forgiveness of ourselves and others we discover a much deeper sense of self-respect and therefore respect of others and of all of life...*

## Journaling and Notes

*The Seventh Moon Phase – Oak Moon – Loves All Things*

## Desires, Goals, and Intentions, for the Coming Month

## Moon Dates August into September

- New Moon in Leo – August 4
- First Quarter Moon in Scorpio – August 12
- Full Moon in Aquarius – August 19/20
- Last Quarter Moon in Gemini – August 26
- New Moon in Virgo – September 2/3

# The Eighth Moon Phase of 2024

## August 2024 / September 2024

## The Tree Lore of Holly and the Eighth Moon She Who Heals

***The inner work of true healing and Soul evolution transforms every aspect of your world for the better.***

This Moon time brings the teachings of Holly, associated with shamanic journeying, rites of passage, transition, and the circle of life, death, and re-birth, all beautifully aligning with the wisdom and teachings of She Who Heals.

Traditionally Holly is associated with Soul evolution and used to be placed on coffins to assist the spirit to pass over with ease. In Tree lore this tree signifies transformation bringing significant shifts from one space of consciousness to another creating a bridge or link between worlds.

The magical teachings of She Who Heals emphasizes the gift of self-responsibility, supporting us to take charge of our own negativity and change our dialogue and thinking patterns into thoughts of health, positivity, and love, enabling us to heal ourselves, and to become a channel of healing for others as well.

I found that during this Moon cycle, I became acutely aware of old wounds that I had never quite managed to resolve and put to rest… I imagine most of you will get where I'm coming from on this one… the stuff that just keeps on popping back up even though you thought you'd put it to bed and walked away for good… this is such a human thing!

In my world situations arrived that peeled back even more layers, showing me clearly what I needed to let go of, release, and move beyond, and in doing this deep inner Soul work I was able to clear and heal at a whole new level, mind, body, and soul… and in doing so I found renewed positivity and vitality. I also came to understand that periods of transition and growth are always accompanied by the process of loss, healing, and re-birth and that the power of the emotions that come with this process should not be underestimated!

Think deep and meaningful and you will be on track this month to embrace a level of learning and growth that will create a stunningly strong and solid foundation to take you forwards… onwards and upwards!

**Orange Calcite.**
**Aligning with the Eighth Moon Phase She Who Heals.**
**Healing and renewed vitality.**

Known as the 'Enhancement Stone', Orange Calcite, like other calcites is said to have powerful healing attributes. Associated with the energy of the Sun and the element of Fire, this stunning crystal is said to realign us with renewed vitality, energizing our primary life force.

In my own experience, I can recommend that if you are struggling to feel the confidence to step into your fullest potential or need some assistance to remove inner blocks to discovering and fulfilling your life's purpose then this stunning crystal brings just the energy needed to support you in this process.

***The inner work of true healing and Soul evolution transforms every aspect of your world for the better.***

## The New Moon – August 4th - 12° 33' Leo

A New Moon in Leo naturally lends itself to wishes that focus on creativity, love and romance, playfulness, generosity, and fun. The energy of a Leo New Moon also supports wishes that enhance your personal passions, your leadership qualities, your exuberance and enthusiasm and your determination, along with anything that will foster and encourage the building of your confidence and your individual self-expression. The outgoing energy of Leo invites celebration and affirmation so in preparation for your New Moon wishes and intentions, take time to acknowledge and validate where you are right now, and all that has led you to this point in your life. Centre yourself in gratitude for all of the learning and the life experiences that have made you who you are. And now... with the turbo charged energy of gratitude, focus on your wishes and intentions for the life that you are manifesting!

If you are looking for romance this is the perfect Moon time to set wishes that invite someone into your world whose heart sings from the same page.
If your world feels like it's all work and no play and you are living to work rather than working to live this is a brilliant Moon time to set wishes that address this imbalance and ask for playfulness, joy, and fun, to flow into your world. And in your intentions, you may want to lay out the actions you intend to follow through with to make this real.

In your New Moon ceremonies write down your 10 wishes and open yourself to receive the guidance that you need to highlight the next steps on your pathway of manifestation. To engage with the New Moon energy at its most powerful, be sure to write your wishes down during the 8 hours following the exact time of the New Moon in your location.

**New Moon Global Timings:**

- Los Angeles, USA — Sun, 4 Aug 2024 at 04:12 PDT
- New York, USA — Sun, 4 Aug 2024 at 07:12 EDT
- Reykjavik, Iceland — Sun, 4 Aug 2024 at 11:12 GMT
- London, UK — Sun, 4 Aug 2024 at 12:12 BST
- Paris, France — Sun, 4 Aug 2024 at 13:12 CEST
- Cape Town, South Africa — Sun, 4 Aug 2024 at 13:12 SAST
- Delhi, India — Sun, 4 Aug 2024 at 16:42 IST
- Perth, Australia — Sun, 4 Aug 2024 at 19:12 AWST
- Tokyo, Japan — Sun, 4 Aug 2024 at 20:12 JST
- Sydney, Australia — Sun, 4 Aug 2024 at 21:12 AEST
- Auckland, New Zealand — Sun, 4 Aug 2024 at 23:12 NZST
- Greenwich Mean Time — Sun, 4 Aug 2024 at 11:12 GMT

## My Ten New Moon Wishes

*The Eighth Moon Phase – Holly Moon – She Who Heals*
*My Wishes and Dreams*

1

2

3

4

5

6

7

8

9

10

## My Ten New Moon Intentions

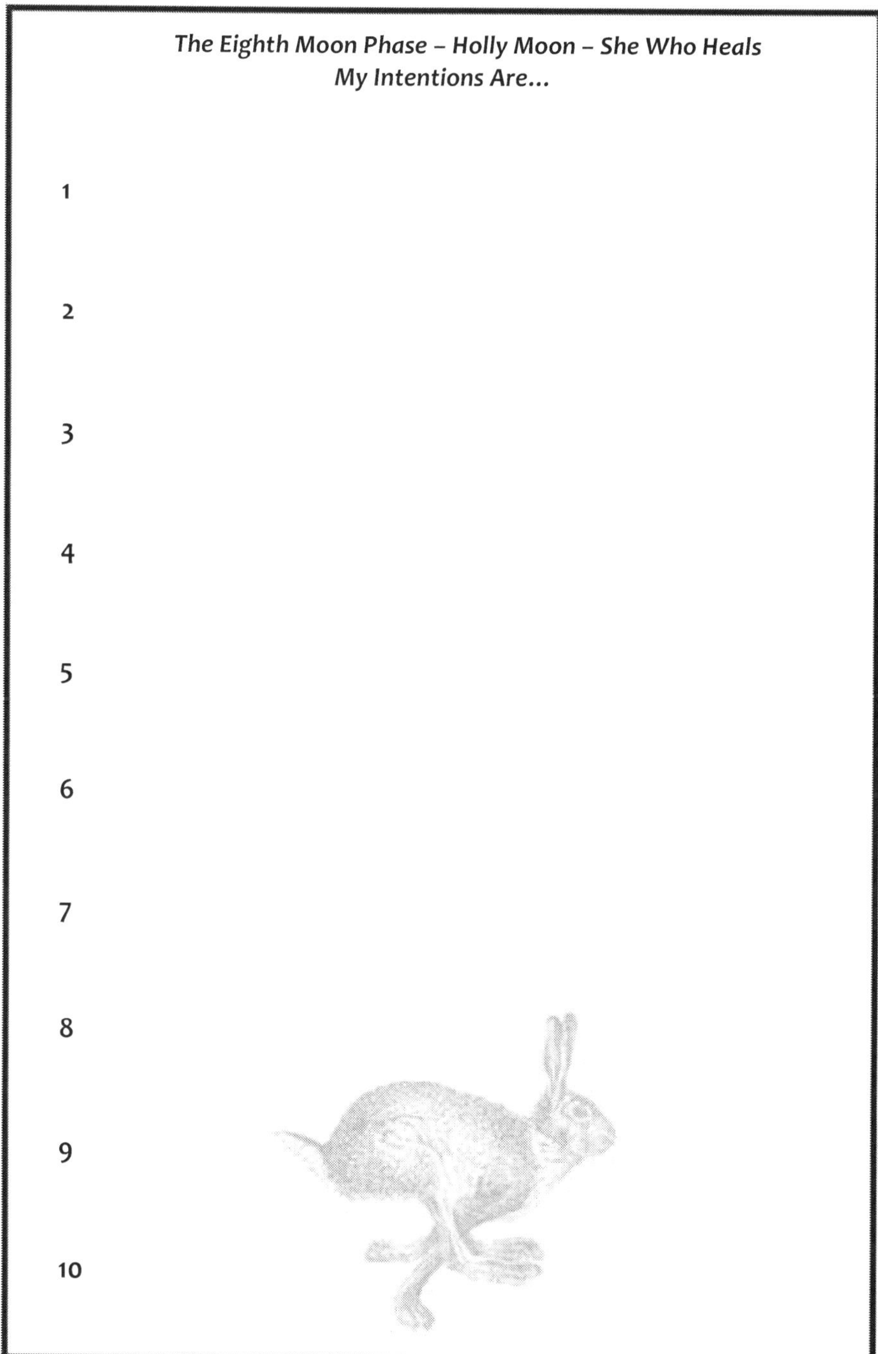

*The Eighth Moon Phase – Holly Moon – She Who Heals*
*My Intentions Are...*

1

2

3

4

5

6

7

8

9

10

## Journaling and Notes

*Think deep and meaningful and you will be on track this month to embrace a level of learning and growth that will create a stunningly strong and solid foundation to take you forwards...*

## My First Quarter Moon Thoughts and Reviews

### The First Quarter Moon – August 12th – Scorpio

*The energy of the Moon is now building and gathering momentum… we see her getting bigger and bigger by the day, so this is a great time to consider how and where you intend to channel and invest this growing expanding energy.*

*Look at where you are in your manifestations and your personal learning. What is showing up in your world right now? What is calling for your attention, and what do you need to prioritize? Where should you apply your greatest focus?*

## The Full Moon – August 19th / 20th - 27° 14' Aquarius

The dynamics of this Full Moon feel seriously full on! Mercury, now in full retrograde motion, sits with the Sun, and there are some very strong, potentially discordant influences taking place, all added to by the Lunar influence.

The themes of Aquarius energy that often show up around the Full Moon relate to friendships and networking, innovation, different ways of seeing things, eccentricity, unexpected results, and heightened awareness of spiritual tools such as astrology, tarot, and other forms of divination.

With all this in mind, during this Moon time be particularly alert to signs signals and synchronicities that bring clarity of direction... even if this information doesn't arrive in the form that you had expected. And also be particularly aware of unexpected conversations and connections that suddenly open up the potential for new ways of seeing, thinking, and doing.

An Aquarius Full Moon naturally illuminates whatever you need to see to help you to fulfil your highest potential, so situations may show up that invite you to re-evaluate, reconsider, and restructure, and where needed, let go of any situations, attitudes, and perceptions that may have been getting in the way of you becoming the very best version of you.

If your schedule allows, take the opportunity to meditate into a space of possibility, this is an amazing Moon time to connect fully with your higher self, and receive guidance that lead to new pathways of consciousness.

Each month place some rainwater or spring water in a bowl and leave it out overnight to absorb the energy of the Full Moon. Do NOT use a plastic bowl! Use glass or earthenware or any container whose fundamental ingredients come from a natural source. Collect the water afterwards and store it in a jar.

Use this Moon Water in any of your ceremonies that hold a higher vision for yourself, others, and humanity as a collective whole, and also any ceremonies that support and further your personal purpose and calling.

**Full Moon Global Timings:**

- Los Angeles, USA — Mon, 19 Aug 2024 at 11:25 PDT
- New York, USA — Mon, 19 Aug 2024 at 14:25 EDT
- Reykjavik, Iceland — Mon, 19 Aug 2024 at 18:25 GMT
- London, UK — Mon, 19 Aug 2024 at 19:25 BST
- Paris, France — Mon, 19 Aug 2024 at 20:25 CEST
- Cape Town, South Africa — Mon, 19 Aug 2024 at 20:25 SAST
- Delhi, India — Mon, 19 Aug 2024 at 23:55 IST
- Perth, Australia — Tue, 20 Aug 2024 at 02:25 AWST
- Tokyo, Japan — Tue, 20 Aug 2024 at 03:25 JST
- Sydney, Australia — Tue, 20 Aug 2024 at 04:25 AEST
- Auckland, New Zealand — Tue, 20 Aug 2024 at 06:25 NZST
- Greenwich Mean Time — Mon, 19 Aug 2024 at 18:25 GMT

## My Full Moon Insights and Illuminations

*The Eighth Moon Phase – Holly Moon – She Who Heals*

## Journaling and Notes

***In Tree lore Holly signifies transformation bringing significant shifts from one space of consciousness to another.***

## My Last Quarter Moon Thoughts and Evaluations

### The Last Quarter Moon – August 26th – Gemini

*The Last Quarter Moon invites you to consolidate your progress and evaluate. Are any unwanted patterns still repeating? Are your plans, actions, and decisions congruent with all that you wish to be and all that you wish to see in the world?*

*The last quarter Moon marks a turning point and a shift in momentum. This is a magnificent time to journal in anticipation of setting clear and deeply personal New Moon wishes and intentions.*

## Journaling and Notes

*Periods of change, transition, and growth are always accompanied by the process of loss, even when the change is desired.*

## Journaling and Notes

*The Eighth Moon Phase – Holly Moon – She Who Heals*

## Desires, Goals, and Intentions, for the Coming Month

## Moon Dates September into October

- New Moon in Virgo – September 2/3
- First Quarter Moon in Sagittarius – September 11
- Full Moon Lunar Eclipse in Pisces – September 17/18
- Autumn Equinox Northern Hemisphere – Spring Equinox Southern Hemisphere – September 22
- Last Quarter Moon in Gemini – September 24
- New Moon Solar Eclipse in Libra – October 2/3

## The Ninth Moon Phase of 2024

### September 2024 / October 2024

### The Tree Lore of Hazel and the Ninth Moon Setting Sun Woman

***Like the Phoenix rising from the ashes, with every phase of our Soul's evolution, we live, we learn, and we grow… stronger and wiser, building a future worthy of generations yet to come.***

The energy of Hazel supports the learning of this Lunar cycle bringing wisdom and inspiration through the magic of divination and prophecy and these teachings align with the values and learning that come from Setting Sun Woman who is the keeper of tomorrows goals and dreams.

For me this period marks a culmination and a turning point of the growth and evolution from the year so far and as I process and move beyond the extraordinary healing and depth of learning gifted in the previous Lunar phase, areas of discord that had previously held me back are finding closure and like an internal harvest of renewed potential, little by little, clarity of direction filters into my mind.

The teachings of Setting Sun Woman honors soul growth and invites you to walk tall and speak your truth beautifully aligning with the lessons and attributes of Hazel. This tree teaches us that we can rise again. Recovery and growth are not only possible, but we can come back with a strength and vigor that surpasses any previous expectations… and with straighter purpose and clearer direction.

A little tree of mighty energy, Hazel understands the true nature of giving and receiving and the value of community. Resilient and durable, this tree knows when to push ahead… when to ease… and when to bend. In my personal experience, sitting with this tree in meditation will put you in touch with your intuitive abilities and bring you creative solutions, showing the best way to respond at any given time. Magic beyond belief!

Whilst I know that there is always more work to be done in the ever-evolving spiral of life, right now, as peace of mind increasingly comes more readily, I find myself humbled in gratitude for all that I have, and mindful to consider my future desires carefully with an awareness that stretches beyond my own lifetime and into the lives of future of generations. With a profound sense of internal peace, I look forwards and anticipate the dreams and promise of the future yet to come.

**Selenite.**
**Aligning with the Ninth Moon Phase Setting Sun Woman.**
**A Moon phase of profound gratitude!**

Selenite draws its name came from Selene, the Greek Goddess of the Moon, and just as the Moon gathers light from the Sun and redistributes it across the Earth, so too Selenite literally embodies and radiates light. This magical and illuminating crystal can be used for healing in its own right or used with other crystals. I personally keep several Selenite sticks and much as I would put my crystals out overnight to re-charge at the Full Moon, I use my selenite sticks to re-charge the energy of my other crystals.

Associated with the alignment of the third eye, crown and etheric chakras, this powerful crystal is a must for anyone seeking Spiritual Guidance. Also known as an Abundance Stone, perhaps a reflection of its generous and giving nature, it is said to connect us with our higher self.

***Like the Phoenix rising from the ashes, with every phase of our Soul's evolution, we live, we learn, and we grow... stronger and wiser...***

## The New Moon – September 2nd / 3rd - 11° 03' Virgo

A New Moon in Virgo lends itself well to areas of life that involve your physical health and wellbeing, your career and workplace, and your ability to be organized and efficient. The Virgo influence also promotes perseverance and a diligent state of mind, being thoughtful to preserve and conserve for a future that stretches beyond your own immediate needs and desires. It also connects to your capacity be discerning within your relationships and hold our boundaries.

This is a fabulous New Moon to wish for the perfect work life balance and if you are looking to manifest a new career pathway the energy of this New Moon will be 100% behind any wishes that invite a career position that aligns you with your greatest contribution. If you are experiencing any form of dissatisfaction, conflict, or challenge, particularly at work with either managers or subordinates, use this New Moon to wish for a balanced resolution that values all parties. If you are someone who is crippled by perfectionism and carries a raging inner critic, use this New Moon to make wishes that ask to release these internal thinking patterns with ease.
To align with the energy of the day and utilize its fullest potential, make a commitment to yourself to honor the validity of your New Moon wishes and declare your commitment to follow through with your New Moon intentions. This is a great Moon time to craft clear affirmations to support you in keeping on track and honoring your continuing progress and in your New Moon ceremonies write down your 10 wishes and open yourself to receive the guidance that you need to highlight the next steps on your pathway of manifestation. To engage with the New Moon energy at its most powerful, be sure to write your wishes down during the 8 hours following the exact time of the New Moon in your location.

**New Moon Global Timings:**

- Los Angeles, USA Mon, 2 Sep 2024 at 18:55 PDT
- New York, USA Mon, 2 Sep 2024 at 21:55 EDT
- Reykjavik, Iceland Tue, 3 Sep 2024 at 01:55 GMT
- London, UK Tue, 3 Sep 2024 at 02:55 BST
- Paris, France Tue, 3 Sep 2024 at 03:55 CEST
- Cape Town, South Africa Tue, 3 Sep 2024 at 03:55 SAST
- Delhi, India Tue, 3 Sep 2024 at 07:25 IST
- Perth, Australia Tue, 3 Sep 2024 at 09:55 AWST
- Tokyo, Japan Tue, 3 Sep 2024 at 10:55 JST
- Sydney, Australia Tue, 3 Sep 2024 at 11:55 AEST
- Auckland, New Zealand Tue, 3 Sep 2024 at 13:55 NZST
- Greenwich Mean Time Tue, 3 Sep 2024 at 01:55 GMT

## My Ten New Moon Wishes

***The Ninth Moon Phase – Hazel Moon – Setting Sun Woman***
***My Wishes and Dreams***

1

2

3

4

5

6

7

8

9

10

## My Ten New Moon Intentions

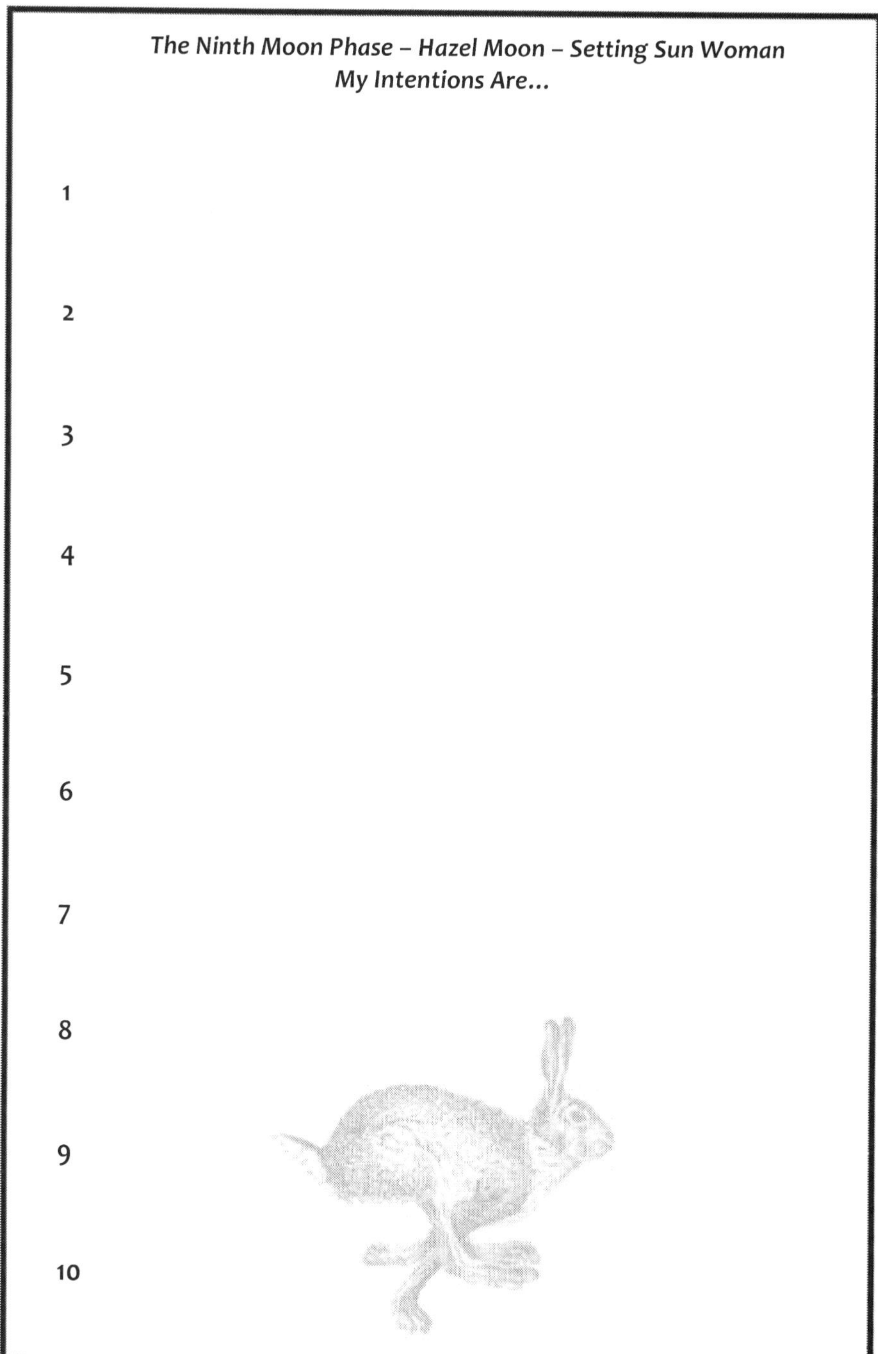

*The Ninth Moon Phase – Hazel Moon – Setting Sun Woman*
*My Intentions Are…*

1

2

3

4

5

6

7

8

9

10

## Journaling and Notes

*Whilst I know that there is always more work to be done in the ever-evolving spiral of life, right now, as peace of mind increasingly comes more readily, I find myself humbled in gratitude for all that I have.*

## My First Quarter Moon Thoughts and Reviews

### The First Quarter Moon – September 11th – Sagittarius

*The energy of the Moon is now building and gathering momentum... we see her getting bigger and bigger by the day, so this is a great time to consider how and where you intend to channel and invest this growing expanding energy.*

*Look at where you are in your manifestations and your personal learning. What is showing up in your world right now? What is calling for your attention, and what do you need to prioritize? Where should you apply your greatest focus?*

## The Full Moon Lunar Eclipse – September 17th / 18th - 25° 40' Pisces

A Full Moon in Pisces will often highlight areas of your world that are still tangled in the past, bringing a window of opportunity to cleanse, release and heal, and given that this is an Eclipse Moon this promises to be a day of significant illumination. Eclipse Season is said to open an energetic portal that enables you to see connections between past actions and present circumstances, to create a point of power in the now. A Piscean Moon is also deeply spiritual, opening channels of communication, so whatever the Full Moon illuminates for you today use this space of heightened intuition to seek divine guidance. The energy of every Full Moon is associated with heightened emotions and the Full Moon in deeply spiritual Pisces is very very emotional so depending on your unique individual circumstances, the flow of emotional energy at this Moon time could bring a flood of dizzy joyous feelings that feel liberating and exhilarating… or… with emotions running high, this could also some more challenging feelings. Now Emotions are actually a part of your natural guidance system, so whatever surfaces today, especially from an emotional perspective, be sure to listen to the underlying voice of those feelings. The Piscean influence will naturally beckon you to find a greater sense of meaning in your life and to connect fully with your spiritual guides, so this is the perfect day to take time out and engage in full on meditation practice with ceremonies that invite illumination and sacred support. Each month place some rainwater or spring water in a bowl and leave it out overnight to absorb the energy of the Full Moon. Do NOT use a plastic bowl! Use glass or earthenware or any container whose fundamental ingredients come from a natural source. Collect the water afterwards and store it in a jar. Use this Moon Water in any of your ceremonies when you need emotional release. It is also perfect to add a power boost in ceremonies that heighten your intuition and psychic abilities and connect you with your Spirit team.

**Full Moon Global Timings:**

- Los Angeles, USA — Tue, 17 Sep 2024 at 19:34 PDT
- New York, USA — Tue, 17 Sep 2024 at 22:34 EDT
- Reykjavik, Iceland — Wed, 18 Sep 2024 at 02:34 GMT
- London, UK — Wed, 18 Sep 2024 at 03:34 BST
- Paris, France — Wed, 18 Sep 2024 at 04:34 CEST
- Cape Town, South Africa — Wed, 18 Sep 2024 at 04:34 SAST
- Delhi, India — Wed, 18 Sep 2024 at 08:04 IST
- Perth, Australia — Wed, 18 Sep 2024 at 10:34 AWST
- Tokyo, Japan — Wed, 18 Sep 2024 at 11:34 JST
- Sydney, Australia — Wed, 18 Sep 2024 at 12:34 AEST
- Auckland, New Zealand — Wed, 18 Sep 2024 at 14:34 NZST
- Greenwich Mean Time — Wed, 18 Sep 2024 at 02:34 GMT

## My Full Moon Insights and Illuminations

*The Ninth Moon Phase – Hazel Moon – Setting Sun Woman*

## Journaling and Notes

*Hazel teaches us that we can rise again. Recovery and growth are not only possible, but we can come back with a strength and vigor that surpasses any previous expectations…*

## My Last Quarter Moon Thoughts and Evaluations

### The Last Quarter Moon – September 24th – Gemini

*The Last Quarter Moon invites you to consolidate your progress and evaluate. Are any unwanted patterns still repeating? Are your plans, actions, and decisions congruent with all that you wish to be and all that you wish to see in the world?*

*The last quarter Moon marks a turning point and a shift in momentum. This is a magnificent time to journal in anticipation of setting clear and deeply personal New Moon wishes and intentions.*

## Journaling and Notes

*There is always more work to be done in the ever-evolving spiral of life, so be mindful to consider the future with an awareness that recognizes the lives of future of generations.*

## Journaling and Notes

*The Ninth Moon Phase – Hazel Moon – Setting Sun Woman*

## Desires, Goals, and Intentions, for the Coming Month

## Moon Dates October into November

- New Moon in Solar Eclipse in Libra – October 2/3
- First Quarter Moon in Capricorn – October 10
- Full Moon in Aries - October 17/18
- Last Quarter Moon in Leo – October 24
- Samhain Northern Hemisphere – Beltane Southern Hemisphere – October 31
- New Moon in Scorpio – November 1/2

## The Tenth Moon Phase of 2024

### October 2024 / November 2024

### The Tree Lore of Vine and the Tenth Moon Weaves the Web

***A time of great creativity and activity... but also of balance... the life you are living and the web you are weaving is the shape of your tomorrow.***

During this Lunar month we are supported by the energy of Vine, representing strength, determination and the bonds of friendship and family aligning with the values and learning from the wisdom of Weaves the Web.

For me the Moon cycle of Weaves the Web always feels like a time to move forwards and embrace the joy of both doing and being and I seem to find that I move into a space of great activity and productivity. I feel connected to the cycle of creation and whether I am persevering to bring existing projects to fruition or sowing new seeds of creative expression, the Lunar energy of this phase seems to help me to renew my motivation and overcome any form of procrastination. There is always more growth to be had but by the time we reach this tenth Moon cycle my internal foundations feel a little bit stronger and I feel that I can walk a little bit taller.

Now although Vine might not technically be considered to be Tree, it nevertheless carries teachings from ancient Tree Lore. Vine grows prolifically and within a fairly short or defined growing season, showing us that productivity has it's time and place, and that resting up is also a natural part of growth and growing. In our western goal driven culture we often only view time as valuable and productive when it is in full forward motion. Vine also then shows us that the bonds of friendship and connectedness are essential to healthy living. Vine grows best on some form of support and if it gets too prolific and grows to fast or too big the very thing that is supporting it will become overloaded and potentially collapse... so in this Moon time we learn that productivity must be respectful of those around us and balanced with relaxation and time to play.

The lessons of Weaves the Web reinforce these messages, reminding us that we can weave webs of resilience and value that stand the test of time... or webs that bind us and restrict, whether these are through internal thinking patterns or actual circumstances, or unhealthy intent such us personal gain and greed at the expense of others. For me this Moon month is a time to honor the balance of both giving and receiving, to share your gifts, and to expand and build the skills you need to make your dreams real and to bring your manifestations into form with awareness of the core values that underpin a world in which all of life can not only survive but thrive.

**Carnelian.**
**Aligning with the Tenth Moon Phase Weaves the Web.**
**A shift in the energy of manifestation.**

Carnelian has to be one of my most favorite Raw Crystals! For me, it is one of those Crystals that does exactly what is says on the tin! The energy of Carnelian is said to restore vitality and bring motivation. Stimulating creativity, it promotes positive life choices.

A powerful crystal of vibrant energy, it is said to bring courage and create a mindset that motivates for success. If you need energy to begin a project or strength and durability to see you through to the finish line, or indeed if you are someone who struggles with a debilitating inner critic that inhibits your perseverance, then this dynamic crystal could become a great friend and ally to you.

***A time of great creativity and activity... but also of balance... the life you are living and the web you are weaving is the shape of your tomorrow.***

## The New Moon Solar Eclipse – October 2nd / 3rd - 10° 03' Libra

A Libra New Moon naturally supports all aspects of balance, harmony, and beauty, especially in your relationships, and that includes your relationship with yourself... and it's eclipse season! In areas of relationship, wishes and intentions made during this Moon time favor themes of co-operation, teamwork, negotiation, tact and diplomacy, equality and appreciation of difference, healthy interdependency and the letting go of unhealthy codependency...

So... if you are someone who struggles to negotiate effectively then this is a fabulous Moon to ask for assistance in releasing any issues around self-value and to request support to develop fluent communications and dealings with others that are fair and equal to all parties, including yourself. If you are seeking long term balance and harmony within relationship and desire marriage and a union of equality then a Libra New Moon is the perfect time to set wishes in this area of your life.

And if any aspect of your health and wellbeing is in need of a rebalance... do your heart and your mind sing from the same page... do you prioritize your own physical health and self-care over the needs of others... this is the perfect Moon to ask for help to realign. If you have never tried Reiki or Chakra energy work but have always wanted to, the Libra influence of this day will give added weight to this kind of mind, body, soul work.

In your New Moon ceremonies write down your 10 wishes and open yourself to receive the guidance that you need to highlight the next steps on your pathway of manifestation. To engage with the New Moon energy at its most powerful, be sure to write your wishes down during the 8 hours following the exact time of the New Moon in your location.

**New Moon Global Timings:**

- Los Angeles, USA — Wed, 2 Oct 2024 at 11:49 PDT
- New York, USA — Wed, 2 Oct 2024 at 14:49 EDT
- Reykjavik, Iceland — Wed, 2 Oct 2024 at 18:49 GMT
- London, UK — Wed, 2 Oct 2024 at 19:49 BST
- Paris, France — Wed, 2 Oct 2024 at 20:49 CEST
- Cape Town, South Africa — Wed, 2 Oct 2024 at 20:49 SAST
- Delhi, India — Thu, 3 Oct 2024 at 00:19 IST
- Perth, Australia — Thu, 3 Oct 2024 at 02:49 AWST
- Tokyo, Japan — Thu, 3 Oct 2024 at 03:49 JST
- Sydney, Australia — Thu, 3 Oct 2024 at 04:49 AEST
- Auckland, New Zealand — Thu, 3 Oct 2024 at 07:49 NZDT
- Greenwich Mean Time — Wed, 2 Oct 2024 at 18:49 GMT

## My Ten New Moon Wishes

***The Tenth Moon Phase – Vine Moon – Weaves the Web***
***My Wishes and Dreams***

1

2

3

4

5

6

7

8

9

10

## My Ten New Moon Intentions

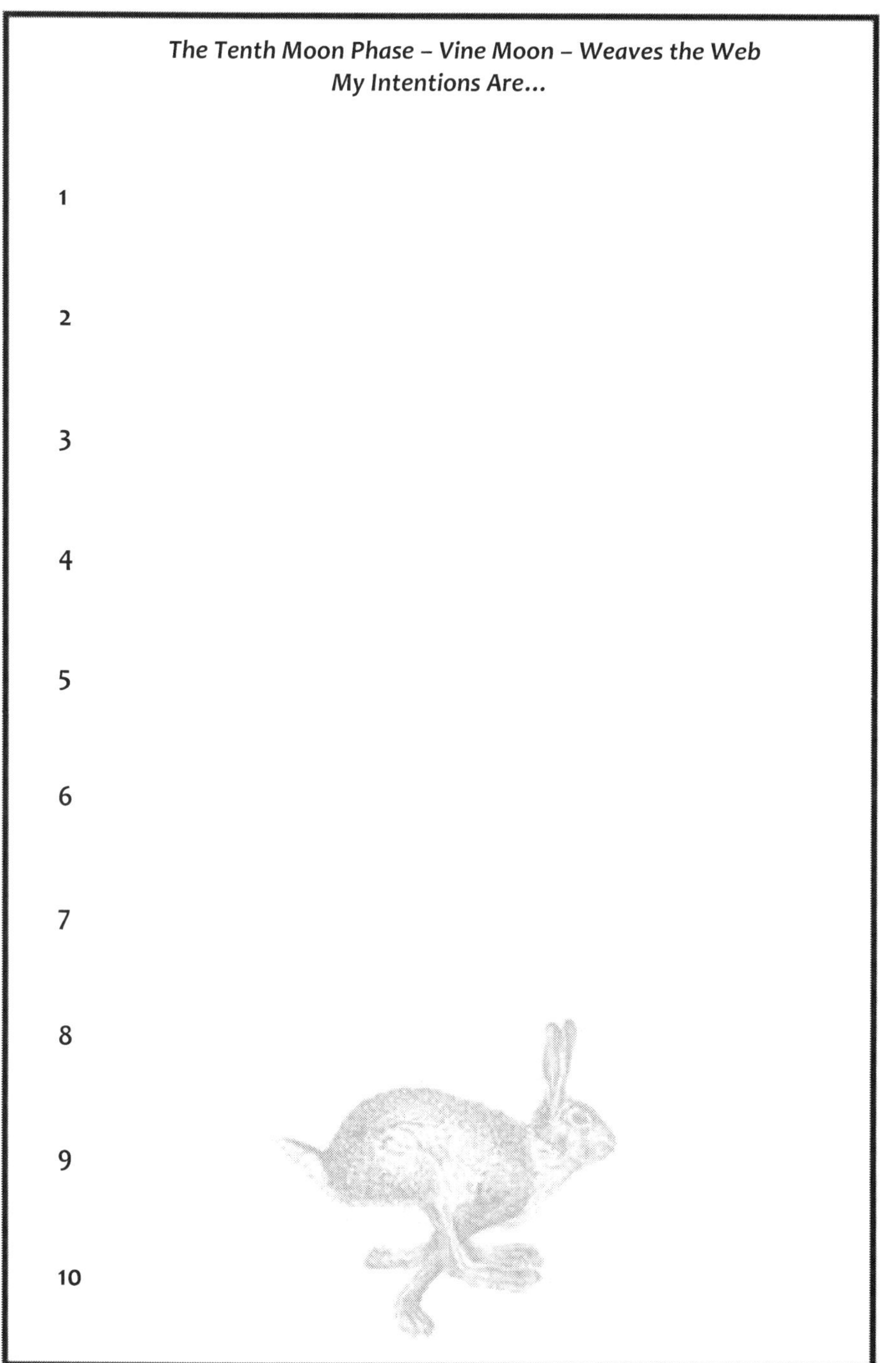

*The Tenth Moon Phase – Vine Moon – Weaves the Web*
*My Intentions Are...*

1

2

3

4

5

6

7

8

9

10

## Journaling and Notes

***The lessons of Weaves the Web remind us that we can weave webs of resilience and value that stand the test of time... or webs that bind us and restrict...***

## My First Quarter Moon Thoughts and Reviews

### The First Quarter Moon – October 10th – Capricorn

*The energy of the Moon is now building and gathering momentum... we see her getting bigger and bigger by the day, so this is a great time to consider how and where you intend to channel and invest this growing expanding energy.*

*Look at where you are in your manifestations and your personal learning. What is showing up in your world right now? What is calling for your attention, and what do you need to prioritize? Where should you apply your greatest focus?*

## The Full Moon – October 17th / 18th - 24° 34' Aries

The Full Moon in Aries ignites passions and fires you up bringing the energy and enthusiasm you need to fuel inject your creative endeavors and rocket them forwards. This truly is a Moon that fosters manifestation in every possible way inviting you to get going and make things happen.

Because an Aries Moon tends to carry a lot of energy it is associated with fiery emotions, so if life is going well you may feel elated and experience a burst of renewed passion and enthusiasm, however in areas of your world that feel uncertain or difficult then emotions could get a little bit intense or challenging. If you think of your emotions as energy-in-motion then this is a Moon time when knowing how to channel emotional energy is a serious asset. If you are struggling with any difficult emotions this book will teach you to understand your emotions as a source of empowerment... even the difficult ones!

***Mindfulness Meets Emotional Awareness, 7 Steps to Learn the Language of your Emotions.***

In terms of ongoing manifestation, this Full Moon promises to illuminate everything that's on track... as well as everything that isn't! And because an Aries Moon naturally lends itself to the initiation of new beginnings, much may be illuminated to show you the way ahead, whether in validation of your ongoing progress, or in validation of a needed change.

Each month place some rainwater or spring water in a bowl and leave it out overnight to absorb the energy of the Full Moon. Do NOT use a plastic bowl! Use glass or earthenware or any container whose fundamental ingredients come from a natural source. Collect the water afterwards and store it in a jar.

Use this Moon Water in any of your ceremonies that are connected to initiating new beginnings, managing strong emotions, or when you need courage to either step into the new, or to hold to your direction with purpose and intent.

**Full Moon Global Timings:**

- Los Angeles, USA Thu, 17 Oct 2024 at 04:26 PDT
- New York, USA Thu, 17 Oct 2024 at 07:26 EDT
- Reykjavik, Iceland Thu, 17 Oct 2024 at 11:26 GMT
- London, UK Thu, 17 Oct 2024 at 12:26 BST
- Paris, France Thu, 17 Oct 2024 at 13:26 CEST
- Cape Town, South Africa Thu, 17 Oct 2024 at 13:26 SAST
- Delhi, India Thu, 17 Oct 2024 at 16:56 IST
- Perth, Australia Thu, 17 Oct 2024 at 19:26 AWST
- Tokyo, Japan Thu, 17 Oct 2024 at 20:26 JST
- Sydney, Australia Thu, 17 Oct 2024 at 22:26 AEDT
- Auckland, New Zealand Fri, 18 Oct 2024 at 00:26 NZDT
- Greenwich Mean Time Thu, 17 Oct 2024 at 11:26 GMT

## My Full Moon Insights and Illuminations

*The Tenth Moon Phase – Vine Moon – Weaves the Web*

## Journaling and Notes

*In this Moon time we learn that productivity must be respectful of those around us and balanced with relaxation and time to play.*

## My Last Quarter Moon Thoughts and Evaluations

### The Last Quarter Moon – October 24th – Leo

*The Last Quarter Moon invites you to consolidate your progress and evaluate. Are any unwanted patterns still repeating? Are your plans, actions, and decisions congruent with all that you wish to be and all that you wish to see in the world?*

*The last quarter Moon marks a turning point and a shift in momentum. This is a magnificent time to journal in anticipation of setting clear and deeply personal New Moon wishes and intentions.*

## Journaling and Notes

***The Moon cycle of Weaves the Web brings a time to move forwards and embrace the joy of both doing and being with a flourish of great activity and productivity.***

## Journaling and Notes

*The Tenth Moon Phase – Vine Moon – Weaves the Web*

## Desires, Goals, and Intentions, for the Coming Month

## Moon Dates November into December

- New Moon in Scorpio – November 1/2
- First Quarter Moon in Aquarius – November 9
- Full Moon in Taurus – 15/16
- Last Quarter Moon in Leo/Virgo – November 22/23
- New Moon in Sagittarius – November 30 / December 1

## The Eleventh Moon Phase of 2024

### November 2024 / December 2024

### The Tree Lore of Ivy and the Eleventh Moon Walks Tall Woman

***Relationships flourish in a mutuality of both giving and receiving and healthy inter-dependency…***

During this Lunar month the values and learning that underpin our personal growth and influence our creative manifestations come from the wisdom of Walks Tall Woman, and the Tree Lore of Ivy, who teaches us how to work together and collaborate in relationship, honoring independence whilst understanding the true nature of healthy interdependence.

Like Vine in the Moon month just past, Ivy too may not technically be described as a tree but still has the wisdom of Tree Lore strongly associated with it. Ivy is a plant that can live in perfect partnership, coexisting and thriving in balanced and equal respect and reverence… however, if not kept in check it can do a serious takeover bid, causing destruction and damage to its counterpart.

These life lessons alongside the teachings of Walks Tall Woman were an absolute revelation to me!

I have been described as fiercely independent and from an early age learned many valuable life skills that meant that I didn't have to depend on anyone and could stand on my own two feet. The situations that showed up in my world during this Moon time helped me to understand the nature of self-sabotage when independence becomes a defense that keeps people out, creating a complete imbalance of giving and receiving. As a consistent over-giver, I needed to significantly review the underlying reasons that caused me to give without discernment, inadvertently creating situations where I welcomed a continuous stream of the wrong kinds of people into my world.

Walks Tall Woman's teachings invite you to stand strong and not be affected by the insecurities of others and she asks you to make a firm commitment to yourself and to understand the difference between healthy pride, when you honor your achievements including your mistakes, as opposed to unhealthy pride, rooted in fear and the hurts of the past, fueling a need to be perfect and approved by everyone, without enquiry or discernment.

I have no doubt that the lessons of this Lunar phase will deepen every year for people like me, gently but firmly removing the patterns within, that have inadvertently fed and reinforced a lack of trust in others.

## Red Calcite.
## Aligning with the Eleventh Moon Phase Walks Tall Woman.
## Discernment, strength, and collaboration.

Red Calcite is associated with an enthusiasm and passion to live life to the full. Full of vitality it enhances and empowers a passion for life, whilst simultaneously grounding and centering, bringing protection and affirming strong boundaries, easing any lethargy or confusion of direction. It is also said to be a major ally when dealing with people who consistently step over our boundaries or have unrealistic expectations as to what and how much we should be giving them! For me, if I find myself trying to spin too many plates at once and I'm going round in circles and not really attending to anything, this powerful stone will help me to put the brakes on without losing any energy. I can then get focused and apply myself to each task with passion and renewed vitality. Associated with the Root Chakra it plays a key role in supporting our capacity for conscious manifestation.

***Relationships flourish in a mutuality of both giving and receiving and healthy inter-dependency...***

## The New Moon – November 1st / 2nd - 9° 34’ Scorpio

A New Moon in Scorpio invites you to dive deep and focus your attention within, letting go of any inner beliefs that limit your potential, whilst leaning into a space of new horizons. This Moon naturally lends its energy to support wishes that focus on empowerment through self-mastery, transformation, the letting go of power struggles, partnerships, deep Soulmate connections and your sensuality and sexuality. Lean into this energetic and use this powerful space to create wishes and intentions that fuel your personal transformation from the inside out. If you are experiencing any kind of inner unease or underlying anxiety but are not sure quite where this is coming from, this is the ideal Moon to ask for help to discover the root cause of any ongoing difficulty, and to be shown exactly what you will need to do to fix these issues.

If you are finding yourself involved in any kind of power struggle, including any internal dilemmas within yourself this is a brilliant New Moon to ask for constructive change, resolution, and if needed, forgiveness. If you are seeking to call in a partner with a depth of Soul connection, mentally, physically, and sexually, then this Moon brings the perfect energy to support this, whilst also helping to remove any internal blocks or insecurities that center around self-doubt and jealousy that may be standing in your way.

In your New Moon ceremonies write down your 10 wishes and open yourself to receive the guidance that you need to highlight the next steps on your pathway of manifestation. To engage with the New Moon energy at its most powerful, be sure to write your wishes down during the 8 hours following the exact time of the New Moon in your location.

**New Moon Global Timings:**

- Los Angeles, USA — Fri, 1 Nov 2024 at 05:46 PDT
- New York, USA — Fri, 1 Nov 2024 at 08:46 EDT
- Reykjavik, Iceland — Fri, 1 Nov 2024 at 12:46 GMT
- London, UK — Fri, 1 Nov 2024 at 12:46 GMT
- Paris, France — Fri, 1 Nov 2024 at 13:46 CET
- Cape Town, South Africa — Fri, 1 Nov 2024 at 14:46 SAST
- Delhi, India — Fri, 1 Nov 2024 at 18:16 IST
- Perth, Australia — Fri, 1 Nov 2024 at 20:46 AWST
- Tokyo, Japan — Fri, 1 Nov 2024 at 21:46 JST
- Sydney, Australia — Fri, 1 Nov 2024 at 23:46 AEDT
- Auckland, New Zealand — Sat, 2 Nov 2024 at 01:46 NZDT
- Greenwich Mean Time — Fri, 1 Nov 2024 at 12:46 GMT

## My Ten New Moon Wishes

*The Eleventh Moon Phase – Ivy Moon – Walks Tall Woman*
*My Wishes and Dreams*

1

2

3

4

5

6

7

8

9

10

# My Ten New Moon Intentions

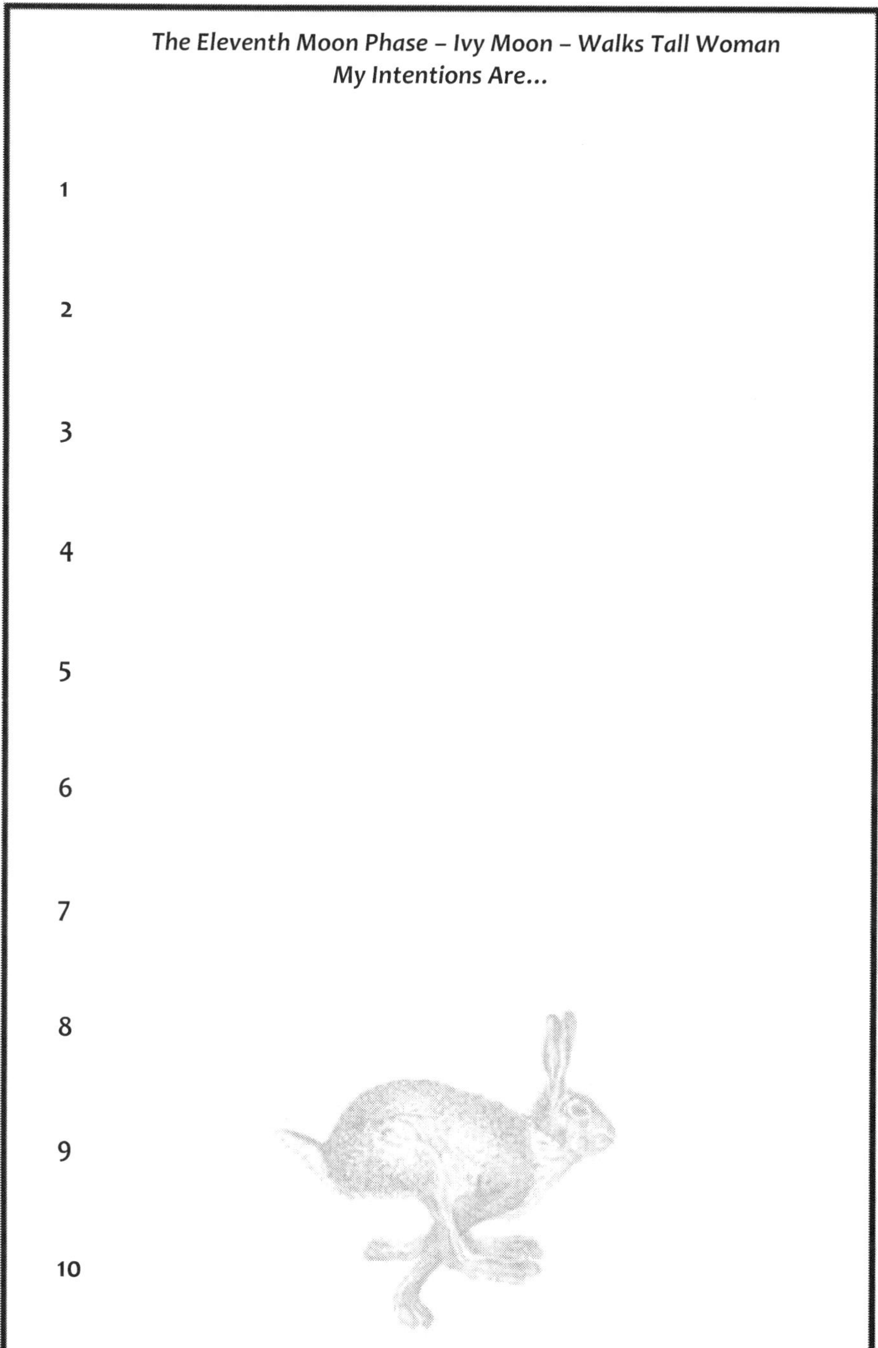

*The Eleventh Moon Phase – Ivy Moon – Walks Tall Woman*
*My Intentions Are…*

1

2

3

4

5

6

7

8

9

10

## Journaling and Notes

*Walks Tall Woman's teachings invite you to stand strong and not be affected by the insecurities of others.*

## My First Quarter Moon Thoughts and Reviews

### The First Quarter Moon – November 9th – Aquarius

*The energy of the Moon is now building and gathering momentum… we see her getting bigger and bigger by the day, so this is a great time to consider how and where you intend to channel and invest this growing expanding energy.*

*Look at where you are in your manifestations and your personal learning. What is showing up in your world right now? What is calling for your attention, and what do you need to prioritize? Where should you apply your greatest focus?*

## The Full Moon – November 15th / 16th - 24° 34' Taurus

A Taurus Moon will naturally focus your attention on security and stability, however, today the Moon is sitting with Uranus, known as the Great Awakener, and this connection can bring an energy that feels erratic and sudden, and pretty much the opposite of everything that we associate with security and stability, so this is going to be a seriously interesting day! This Moon time may well bring to light any insecurities that need attending to, particularly around home, family, finances, your physical and sensual appearance, and your health. And this will include the health of your self-esteem and emotional wellness as well.

If during this Moon time you find yourself wanting to stay at home and retreat, then listen to this calling and go to ground. You may need to rest up and replenish before ploughing ahead again. The energy of a Taurus Full Moon can bring perseverance and inspire you to push forwards, regardless of any obstacles in your path and as a general rule, when your actions are in pursuit of higher ideals, the energy flow will work for you bringing staying power and stamina, however, the fired up version of Taurus energy can feel like a bull in a china shop, pushing through without thought or regard and so this Moon will also highlight aspects of your world where you may need to slow down, take it a bit more easy, steady your pace, and maybe even tread a little more lightly.

Each month place some rainwater or spring water in a bowl and leave it out overnight to absorb the energy of the Full Moon. Do NOT use a plastic bowl! Use glass or earthenware or any container whose fundamental ingredients come from a natural source. Collect the water afterwards and store it in a jar.

Use this Moon Water in any of your ceremonies where you need to find perseverance and staying power, or perhaps to slow something down to a manageable pace bringing slow and steady progress

**Full Moon Global Timings:**

- Los Angeles, USA — Fri, 15 Nov 2024 at 13:28 PST
- New York, USA — Fri, 15 Nov 2024 at 16:28 EST
- Reykjavik, Iceland — Fri, 15 Nov 2024 at 21:28 GMT
- London, UK — Fri, 15 Nov 2024 at 21:28 GMT
- Paris, France — Fri, 15 Nov 2024 at 22:28 CET
- Cape Town, South Africa — Fri, 15 Nov 2024 at 23:28 SAST
- Delhi, India — Sat, 16 Nov 2024 at 02:58 IST
- Perth, Australia — Sat, 16 Nov 2024 at 05:28 AWST
- Tokyo, Japan — Sat, 16 Nov 2024 at 06:28 JST
- Sydney, Australia — Sat, 16 Nov 2024 at 08:28 AEDT
- Auckland, New Zealand — Sat, 16 Nov 2024 at 10:28 NZDT
- Greenwich Mean Time — Fri, 15 Nov 2024 at 21:28 GMT

## My Full Moon Insights and Illuminations

*The Eleventh Moon Phase – Ivy Moon – Walks Tall Woman*

## Journaling and Notes

*This Moon teaches collaboration in relationship, honoring independence whilst understanding the true nature of healthy interdependence.*

## My Last Quarter Moon Thoughts and Evaluations

### The Last Quarter Moon – November 22nd / 23rd – Leo / Virgo

*The Last Quarter Moon invites you to consolidate your progress and evaluate. Are any unwanted patterns still repeating? Are your plans, actions, and decisions congruent with all that you wish to be and all that you wish to see in the world?*

*The last quarter Moon marks a turning point and a shift in momentum. This is a magnificent time to journal in anticipation of setting clear and deeply personal New Moon wishes and intentions.*

## Journaling and Notes

***Independence and even giving can become a shield that keeps people at a distance, fueling an imbalance of giving and receiving.***

## Journaling and Notes

*The Eleventh Moon Phase – Ivy Moon – Walks Tall Woman*

## Desires, Goals, and Intentions, for the Coming Month

## Moon Dates December

- New Moon in Sagittarius – November 30 / December 1
- First Quarter Moon in Pisces – December 8
- Full Moon in Gemini – December 15
- Winter Solstice Northern Hemisphere – Summer Solstice Southern Hemisphere – December 21
- Last Quarter Moon in Virgo/Libra – December 22/23
- New Moon in Capricorn – December 30/31

## The Twelfth Moon Phase of 2024

### December 2024

### The Tree Lore of Reed and the Twelfth Moon Gives Praise

**Your physical body, your thoughts, your feelings, and emotions... are all actively involved in the process of creation every minute of the day!**

This Moon month we are supported by the teachings of Reed and the tribal teachings of the Clan Moon Mother, Gives Praise. The teachings of Reed are associated with rising above the ego mind and aligning your desires with the wisdom of your higher self. In essence... as above so below... with you yourself being the vessel of connection and manifestation of those higher minded desires into form and Gives Praise teaches us about the magic of congruence and authenticity. By becoming who and what we wish to see in the world and through living the essence of those values, we then attract more of the same.

Let's look at the symbolism of Reed first. For me, the most magical element of Reeds ancient wisdom is that if you spend time by a Reed bed and get really still, when the wind is just right they will sing! And in Celtic traditions this was thought to be a voice from the otherworld's and a significant connection that brought messages from Spirit. Reeds were also used as roofing and so were therefore associated with protection, and also used for flooring, as they give off a faint but glorious smell and so were considered to have cleansing and purifying properties.

I think the lessons of this Lunar phase embody the very essence of what manifestation is truly about. During this Moon time so many situations, some small and some very big, seemed to miraculously appear in my world, demonstrating so clearly that abundance comes to us from the inside out and is massively influenced by our perceptions, attitudes, and state of mind. During this Moon cycle I became very conscious of the inner workings of my internal dialogue. It is so easy to present the universe with wishes and desires whilst simultaneously holding many internal negative thoughts and beliefs that can continually replay in the background without us realizing how much air play they are taking up! Negative thoughts magnetize and magnify difficulties whilst gratitude magnetizes and attracts abundance.

It is also such a human thing to hold really good values and yet not really step up to the mark and see them through into our actions. The power and magic of abundance is having the right attitude... and meaning it... and knowing it... and being it... and doing it! This is congruence, and the core recipe for success and abundance.

**Rainbow Fluorite.**
**Aligning with the Twelfth Moon Phase Gives Praise**
**The laws of attraction!**

Fluorite comes in many colors and is known as a great emotional stabilizer. It puts the breaks on when our mind races and we feel ourselves spiraling into emotional overload. Bringing our chakras into alignment in a very particular way it is said to allow us to see our situation through a different lens. As such it is a major helper if we suffer from habitual thinking patterns that cloud our judgement and block us from approaching our situation in a grounded and realistic manner.

Rainbow fluorite is said to be particularly helpful in work settings where we feel easily overloaded. Simply holding this crystal for a short while will bring clarity and calm releasing any emotional toxicity that may cloud our judgement.

**Your physical body, your thoughts, your feelings, and emotions... are all actively involved in the process of creation every minute of the day!**

## The New Moon – November 30th / December 1st - 9° 32' Sagittarius

The Lunar influence of this New Moon beautifully support the setting of wishes and intentions that infuse any and all of your manifestations with enthusiasm, renewed faith and optimism, positive expectations, and the finding of solutions to expand your horizons, surrounding your hopes and dreams with positivity, determination, and grace. Themes surrounding the Sagittarius influence also include spontaneity and adventure, integrity, ethics and honesty, philosophy, good luck, and generosity, and so this Moon time brings a natural flow of energy that aligns with renewed hope, helping to overcome depression, and form a connection with higher minded ideals and the finding of solutions.

If you are seeking spontaneity and adventure and have been searching to find a purpose that feels inspirational and really floats your boat then this is a perfect Moon to set wishes that request signposts to show you what steps to take next to bring a clarity of direction easily and quickly. The Sagittarius vibe will also enhance any wishes that connect with your personal sense of freedom, the rights and freedom of others, truth, liberty, and justice.

Wishes set at this time are primed to bring increased motivation, with stamina and determination to see something through, so if you have ever struggled with procrastination, then this is also the perfect New Moon to request that these thinking patterns leave you and are easily let go of.

In your New Moon ceremonies write down your 10 wishes and open yourself to receive the guidance that you need to highlight the next steps on your pathway of manifestation. To engage with the New Moon energy at its most powerful, be sure to write your wishes down during the 8 hours following the exact time of the New Moon in your location.

**New Moon Global Timings:**

- Los Angeles, USA — Sat, 30 Nov 2024 at 22:21 PST
- New York, USA — Sun, 1 Dec 2024 at 01:21 EST
- Reykjavik, Iceland — Sun, 1 Dec 2024 at 06:21 GMT
- London, UK — Sun, 1 Dec 2024 at 06:21 GMT
- Paris, France — Sun, 1 Dec 2024 at 07:21 CET
- Cape Town, South Africa — Sun, 1 Dec 2024 at 08:21 SAST
- Delhi, India — Sun, 1 Dec 2024 at 11:51 IST
- Perth, Australia — Sun, 1 Dec 2024 at 14:21 AWST
- Tokyo, Japan — Sun, 1 Dec 2024 at 15:21 JST
- Sydney, Australia — Sun, 1 Dec 2024 at 17:21 AEDT
- Auckland, New Zealand — Sun, 1 Dec 2024 at 19:21 NZDT
- Greenwich Mean Time — Sun, 1 Dec 2024 at 06:21 GMT

## My Ten New Moon Wishes

***The Twelfth Moon Phase – Reed Moon – Gives Praise***
***My Wishes and Dreams***

1

2

3

4

5

6

7

8

9

10

## My Ten New Moon Intentions

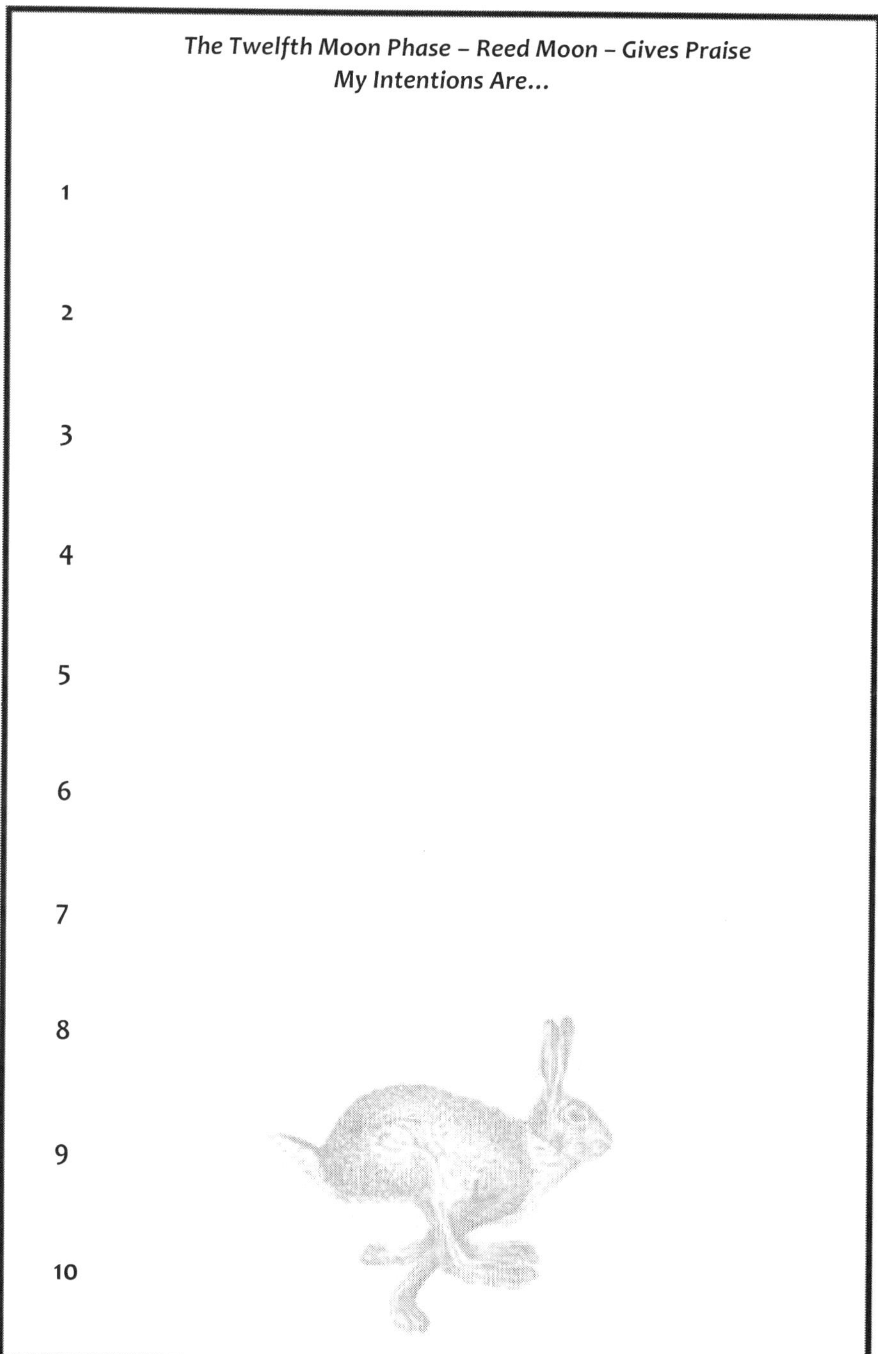

*The Twelfth Moon Phase – Reed Moon – Gives Praise*
*My Intentions Are...*

1

2

3

4

5

6

7

8

9

10

## Journaling and Notes

*Gives Praise teaches us about the magic of congruence and authenticity. By becoming who and what we wish to see in the world and through living the essence of those values, we then attract more of the same.*

## My First Quarter Moon Thoughts and Reviews

### The First Quarter Moon – December 8th – Pisces

*The energy of the Moon is now building and gathering momentum... we see her getting bigger and bigger by the day, so this is a great time to consider how and where you intend to channel and invest this growing expanding energy.*

*Look at where you are in your manifestations and your personal learning. What is showing up in your world right now? What is calling for your attention, and what do you need to prioritize? Where should you apply your greatest focus?*

## The Full Moon – December 15th - 23° 52' Gemini

A Gemini Moon governs areas of the personality and development that connects to learning, reading, writing, speaking, listening, and all areas of communication. The Full Moon in Gemini will naturally illuminate any aspects of your world that can be extended, grown, and developed further, to enhance better and more fluent communication, whether with yourself or with others. This Moon may also highlight any internal contradictions in your thinking patterns and behaviors and through this awareness, create an avenue of healing and resolution.
Whatever is taking place in your world at this time, this Moon time will often illuminate all aspects of a situation and show both sides of the story… and whilst on occasion this can create confusion or indecision, the value of this influence is to give you the opportunity to see things clearly and then with full awareness you can then make conscious choices and decisions.
To use this energy at its best, rather than engaging in any fast and furious re-actions, take time to reflect before responding. If you find yourself experiencing heightened positive emotions then ride the waves and enjoy… however, if you find yourself experiencing heightened negative emotions then press the pause button and take a minute's silence to re-anchor yourself, and then review all aspects of your situation before moving forwards.
Each month place some rainwater or spring water in a bowl and leave it out overnight to absorb the energy of the Full Moon. Do NOT use a plastic bowl! Use glass or earthenware or any container whose fundamental ingredients come from a natural source. Collect the water afterwards and store it in a jar.
Use this Moon Water in any of your ceremonies where you need to step back and understand all sides of the story, calm your mental energy, or find clarity of vision and a clear way forward.

**Full Moon Global Timings:**

- Los Angeles, USA — Sun, 15 Dec 2024 at 01:01 PST
- New York, USA — Sun, 15 Dec 2024 at 04:01 EST
- Reykjavik, Iceland — Sun, 15 Dec 2024 at 09:01 GMT
- London, UK — Sun, 15 Dec 2024 at 09:01 GMT
- Paris, France — Sun, 15 Dec 2024 at 10:01 CET
- Cape Town, South Africa — Sun, 15 Dec 2024 at 11:01 SAST
- Delhi, India — Sun, 15 Dec 2024 at 14:31 IST
- Perth, Australia — Sun, 15 Dec 2024 at 17:01 AWST
- Tokyo, Japan — Sun, 15 Dec 2024 at 18:01 JST
- Sydney, Australia — Sun, 15 Dec 2024 at 20:01 AEDT
- Auckland, New Zealand — Sun, 15 Dec 2024 at 22:01 NZDT
- Greenwich Mean Time — Sun, 15 Dec 2024 at 09:01 GMT

## My Full Moon Insights and Illuminations

*The Twelfth Moon Phase – Reed Moon – Gives Praise*

## Journaling and Notes

*The lessons of Reed teach you to rise above the ego mind and align your desires with the wisdom of your higher self, in essence... as above so below...*

## My Last Quarter Moon Thoughts and Evaluations

### The Last Quarter Moon – December 22nd / 23rd – Virgo / Libra

*The Last Quarter Moon invites you to consolidate your progress and evaluate. Are any unwanted patterns still repeating? Are your plans, actions, and decisions congruent with all that you wish to be and all that you wish to see in the world?*

*The last quarter Moon marks a turning point and a shift in momentum. This is a magnificent time to journal in anticipation of setting clear and deeply personal New Moon wishes and intentions.*

## Journaling and Notes

*The power and magic of abundance is having the right attitude... and meaning it... and knowing it... and being it... and doing it! This is congruence, and the core recipe for success and abundance.*

## Journaling and Notes

*The Twelfth Moon Phase – Reed Moon – Gives Praise*

## Desires, Goals, and Intentions, for the Coming Month

## Moon Dates December 2024 into January 2025

- New Moon in Capricorn – December 30/31
- First Quarter Moon in Aries – January 6/7 - 2025
- Full Moon in Cancer – January 13
- Last Quarter Moon in Libra/Scorpio – January 21/22 – 2025
- First New Moon of 2025 is in Aquarius – January 29

## The Thirteenth Moon Phase of 2024 moving into 2025

### December 2024 / January 2025

### The Tree Lore of Elder and the Thirteenth Moon Becomes Her Vision

***In the Stillness your Soul calls for Unity, Wholeness, and a Vision for the Future.***

We end this year with the Thirteenth Moon Phase of Becomes Her Vision. This Moon is aligned with the energy of Elder. In Tree Lore, she is the grandmother of trees and the keeper of the divine feminine. Traditional folk stories say that if you sleep under an Elder Tree at night you will journey between the worlds and see the Truth in all things... including the truth of yourself! We do not always get thirteen Moon in a year and as this Moon time is so close to the handover into 2025 the teachings will almost certainly mix and merge with those of the First Moon Phase of 2025, Talks with Relations, and the Tree Lore of Birch.

This is a time to integrate your learning from the previous twelve Moons in preparation for a new cycle of Soul growth and personal evolution. This Moon invites you to face yourself in all your wonderful humanness, your ups, and your downs... and from a place of profound honesty, look back over the previous year. So, celebrate all the good stuff but also take time to notice the things that you would like to be different. When we set New Year resolutions, we often list the things that we intend to give up so we can free ourselves from limiting habits. The influence of this Moon is here to show you what you need to see so that you can then attend to the details and move beyond previous limitations. I see it as entering a month long spiritual therapy session with a wonderfully compassionate and yet very tough therapist who is prepared to hold me to account knowing that facing myself will become the greatest source of my empowerment.

If you are someone who tends to pick yourself to pieces then please don't! Noticing is always the starting point of any form of conscious change... and for a human life to be lived to the fullest, there will be many challenges... but at a level of Soul growth, each and every one is an entry point into newer and higher levels of consciousness! Learning to live through conscious choice with awareness of our contribution to the whole involves a lifetime of study... so enjoy the journey. For me this Moon time is a humbling reminder that how we each live radiates beyond the immediacy of our own lives, affecting all who we come into contact with and also stretching into the future, impacting on generations yet to come. When we embrace the pathway to wholeness through individual expression and yet also strive for oneness, the illusion of separateness disappears in the face of the truth and love of all prevails.

**Rose Quartz.**
**Aligning with the Thirteenth Moon Phase Becomes her Vision.**
**The highest vibration of love.**

Rose Quartz is a stone of universal love. It is said to restore trust and to bring about peace and harmony, healing relationship wounds not only between ourselves and others but also in our relationship with ourselves.

Its highest vibration of love is said to encourage unconditional love in all forms, its energy purifying and opening the heart Chakra, promoting love, self-love, friendship, deep inner healing, and feelings of peace. It is also said to dispel negativity and protect against any form of environmental pollution, including the negative energy and attitudes of other people around you, replacing it with loving vibrations.

***In the Stillness your Soul calls for Unity, Wholeness, and a Vision for the Future.***

## The New Moon – December 30th / 31st - 9° 43' Capricorn

A Capricorn New Moon always falls in the period of the end of December through into the beginning of January and so this is perfect Moon for making wishes that focus on your New Year resolutions and intentions. Capricorn energy naturally focuses on ambitions, goals, and personal desires for success and recognition and so in your preparations for this Moon time you may want to ask yourself what really matters to you, and what have you learned from the previous year, and what do you wish to focus on and manifest in the year ahead?

The energetics of this New Moon are gorgeous and arrive like a breath of fresh air, and the overall underlying dynamics are primed for renewal and rebirth flowing from a space of genuine desire that is rooted in understanding and conscious awareness. This is lovely! This is a New Moon that invites you to energetically set the pace for the coming year of 2025 and to not only dream big... but dream bold... and dream ambitious... and then be prepared to step up and follow through. Not just in the immediacy of now, but right through the coming year. Manifestation is not just a process of putting a request into the universe and assuming it will arrive. Manifestation involves having an awareness of a bigger picture and your personal interconnectedness with all of life. And then, alongside placing your requests into the Universe, embodying the very essence of all that you wish to manifest for yourself and indeed all that you wish to see in the world... and then, whilst consistently upholding these core values, simultaneously opening yourself to receive. So get to it!
In your New Moon ceremonies write down your 10 wishes and open yourself to receive the guidance that you need to highlight the next steps on your pathway of manifestation. To engage with the New Moon energy at its most powerful, be sure to write your wishes down during the 8 hours following the exact time of the New Moon in your location.

**New Moon Global Timings:**

- Los Angeles, USA — Mon, 30 Dec 2024 at 14:26 PST
- New York, USA — Mon, 30 Dec 2024 at 17:26 EST
- Reykjavik, Iceland — Mon, 30 Dec 2024 at 22:26 GMT
- London, UK — Mon, 30 Dec 2024 at 22:26 GMT
- Paris, France — Mon, 30 Dec 2024 at 23:26 CET
- Cape Town, South Africa — Tue, 31 Dec 2024 at 00:26 SAST
- Delhi, India — Tue, 31 Dec 2024 at 03:56 IST
- Perth, Australia — Tue, 31 Dec 2024 at 06:26 AWST
- Tokyo, Japan — Tue, 31 Dec 2024 at 07:26 JST
- Sydney, Australia — Tue, 31 Dec 2024 at 09:26 AEDT
- Auckland, New Zealand — Tue, 31 Dec 2024 at 11:26 NZDT
- Greenwich Mean Time — Mon, 30 Dec 2024 at 22:26 GMT

## My Ten New Moon Wishes

***The Thirteenth Moon Phase 2024/2025 - Elder Moon - Becomes Her Vision***
***My Wishes and Dreams***

1

2

3

4

5

6

7

8

9

10

# My Ten New Moon Intentions

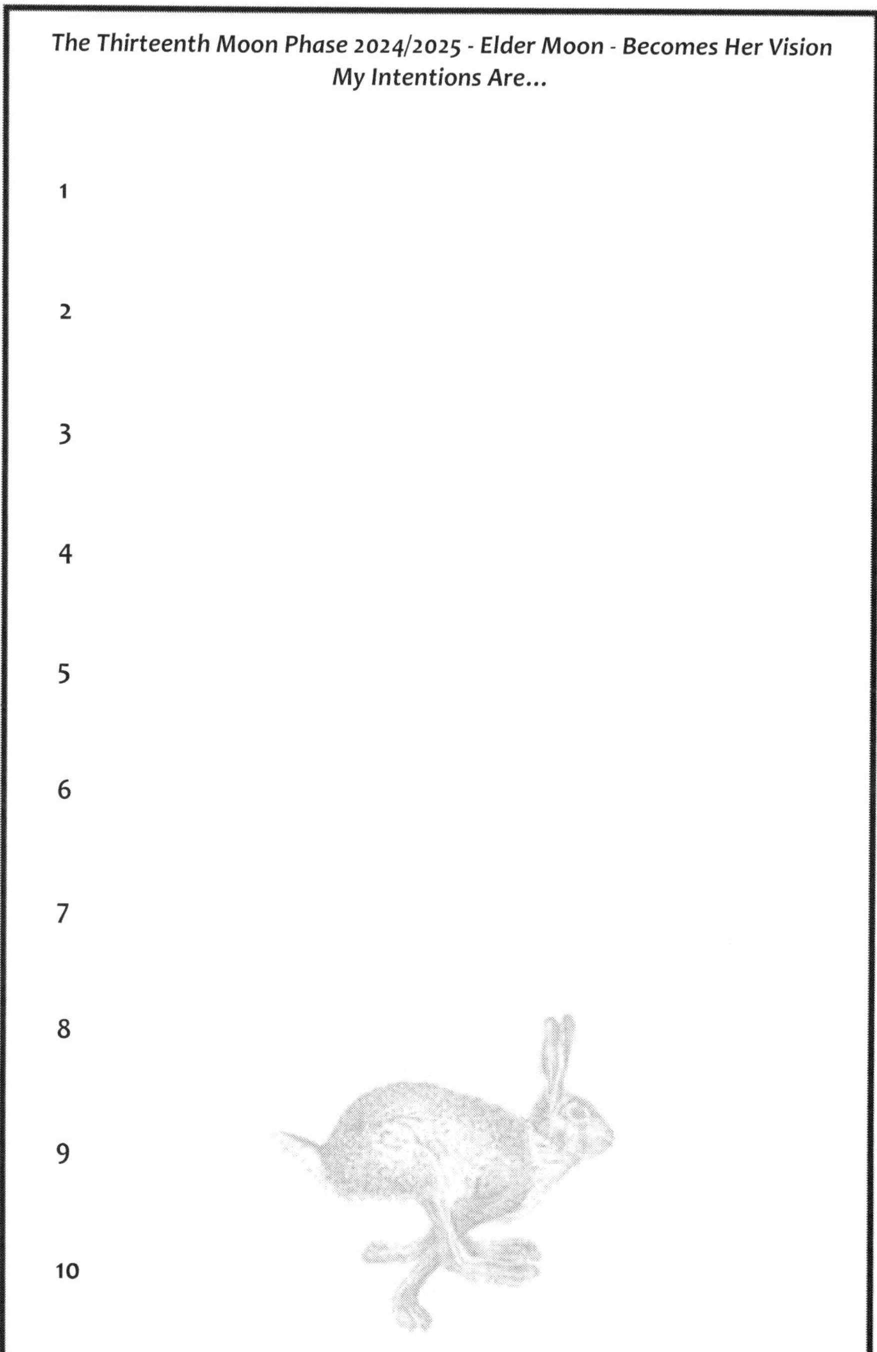

*The Thirteenth Moon Phase 2024/2025 - Elder Moon - Becomes Her Vision*
*My Intentions Are...*

1

2

3

4

5

6

7

8

9

10

## Journaling and Notes

***This is a time to integrate your learning from the previous twelve Moons in preparation for a new cycle of Soul growth and personal evolution.***

## Journaling and Notes

*Learning to live through conscious choice with awareness of your contribution to the whole involves a lifetime of study... so enjoy the journey...*

## Desires, Goals, and Intentions, for 2025

*Every life experience, the good, the bad and everything in between, is actually an entry point into newer and higher levels of consciousness.*

**Happy Moon Manifesting in 2025!**

## Book Recommendations

### Moon Books

The 13 Original Clan Mothers – Jamie Sams
Earth Medicine – Jamie Sams
New Moon Astrology – Jan Spiller
Lunar Living – Kirsty Gallagher

### Tree Books

Walking With Trees – Glennie kindred
The Hidden Life of Trees – Wohlleben

### Science, Energy, Mind Body & Soul

Eastern Body Western Mind – Anodea Judith
The Body Keeps the Score – Bessel van der Kolk
The Field – Lynne McTaggart
The Intention Experiment - Lynne McTaggart
The Hidden Messages in Water – Masuro Emoto
The Biology of Belief – Bruce Lipton
Spiritual Intelligence – Danah Zohar & Ian Marshall
Soul Retrieval – Sandra Ingerman

## About the Author

Jenny Florence is a best-selling Author. Her career as a professional Accredited BACP, UKRC Registered Counsellor spanned over 28 years working with individuals, couples, and teams.

She is the founder and creator of the A-Z of Emotional Health on-line Video Library, a free Public Resource, dedicated to understanding Emotional and Mental Wellness from a holistic perspective.

She first began reading Tarot cards as a teenager and has also studied astrology.

For more information visit her Free on-line Library; https://www.azemotionalhealth.com/

Her books and cards include:

- 7 Steps to Spiritual Empathy – Learn to Listen, Change your Life!
- Mindfulness meets Emotional Awareness - 7 Steps to Learn the Language of your Emotions
- I Choose Love – the A-Z Guidebook for the Spiritual Warrior
- Manifest with the Moon Astro-Moon Diary and Journal
- The Art of Manifestation Oracle Cards.

You can order her books and cards via your local bookstore or from Amazon.

To watch free monthly tutorials and support Jenny's ongoing work join Patreon

- https://www.patreon.com/AZEmotionalHealth

To access Lunar updates, Webinars, and Readings follow Jenny on social media.

- https://www.youtube.com/c/MoonMagicWeeklyTarot
- https://www.facebook.com/MoonMagicJennyFlorence
- https://www.instagram.com/moonmagicjennyflorence/

Made in the USA
Columbia, SC
13 April 2024